Poetry & Strikes

Poetry & ...

Series Editors

Ralph Pite *University of Bristol*
Deryn Rees-Jones *University of Liverpool*

Series Board

Peter Barry *Aberystwyth University*
Neil Corcoran *University of Liverpool*
James Longenbach *University of Rochester, USA*
Jan Montefiore *University of Kent*
Barbara Page *Vassar College, USA*
Marjorie Perloff *Stanford University, USA*
Adam Piette *University of Sheffield*
Stan Smith *Nottingham Trent University*

Also in this series

Poetry & Displacement Stan Smith
Poetry & Language Writing David Arnold
Poetry & Translation: The Art of the Impossible Peter Robinson
Science in Modern Poetry John Holmes
Poetry & Geography Edited by Neal Alexander and David Cooper
Poetry & Responsibility Neil Corcoran
Poetry & Barthes Calum Gardner
Poetry & the Dictionary Edited by Andrew Blades and Piers Pennington
Poetry & Money: Speculation Peter Robinson
Poetry & Commons: Postwar and Romantic Lyric in Times of Enclosure Daniel Eltringham

Poetry & Strikes

Trade Union Narratives and Legacies

Michael James

LIVERPOOL UNIVERSITY PRESS

First published 2023 by
Liverpool University Press
4 Cambridge Street
Liverpool
L69 7ZU

Copyright © 2023 Michael James

Michael James has asserted the right to be identified as the author of this book in accordance with the Copyright, Designs and Patents Act 1988.

All rights reserved. No part of this book may be reproduced, stored in a retrieval system, or transmitted, in any form or by any means, electronic, mechanical, photocopying, recording, or otherwise, without the prior written permission of the publisher.

Trademark notice: Product or corporate names may be trademarks or registered trademarks, and are used only for identification and explanation without intent to infringe.

British Library Cataloguing-in-Publication data
A British Library CIP record is available

ISBN 978-1-80085-540-3 cased

Typeset by Carnegie Book Production, Lancaster
Printed and bound by CPI Group (UK) Ltd, Croydon CR0 4YY

Contents

Acknowledgements		vii
Introduction: Introducing Poetry and Strikes		1
1	How Did We Get Here? The History	23
2	Unions and Not Unions	35
3	Naming Scargills and Thatchers	65
4	Strikes and Place	91
5	Other Poetic Responses	109
Conclusion		125
Bibliography		131
Index		141

Acknowledgements

This book is dedicated to my dad, John James. While he isn't here to read it, it wouldn't exist without him. To my mum, Barbara, for backing me throughout.

To Anna, who has always seen the value in this work and whose conversation and support allowed it to flourish. To Kit, for being completely yourself, always.

Thanks to those who gave me feedback on earlier drafts of this book, to those who have answered questions, to those who have provided information and given their time, and those who helped me along the way. Thank you for thinking these things matter.

Many thanks go to Steve Ely and Smokestack Books for granting permission to reproduce quotations from Ely's work in this book.

Finally, thank you to everyone involved in the trade union movement for continuing to believe that we can, and should, expect better.

Introduction: Introducing Poetry and Strikes

> You can't write a political poem if it is just about politics.
> Nick Laird, *The Irish Times* (2005)

In a lecture given in 1996, Terry Eagleton claimed that 'politics is a local transient business in which a week is a long time, whereas poetry, or at least the better sort, is universal and enduring' (Eagleton in Battersby 1996, n.pag.). Eagleton's assertion sets a binary between poetry and politics that implies a poetry which can only speak to the underlying, 'universal' concerns that politics raises, not to political action itself. Eagleton suggests that our politics is always new, that it is continually moving, with last week's political concerns relegated or replaced by what is current, and therefore important. Eagleton does not consider that politics leaves a trail, that while the conversation may change, the political focus may shift, it creates a legacy. He continues by saying that 'politics is a question of abstract notions, impersonal institutions, collective entities. Politics involves well defined, determinant ideas, whereas poetry thrives on indeterminacy and ambiguity' (Eagleton in Battersby 1996, n.pag.). For Eagleton, politics is the abstract and detached made real. Politics involves the *appearance* of well-defined ideas and the *attempted* control of these determinant ideas through which to fashion certain political narratives. While poetry does indeed trade on linguistic ambiguity, to call it an 'indeterminacy' is to neglect the formal establishment, arrangement and content of a poem. Poetry calls into question the 'determinant ideas' presented to us by political institutions and the groups that seek to control our narratives. These types of narrative are particularly powerful in shaping our labour histories and the legacies they create.

In terms of labour representation and strike histories in particular, how narratives are told and our legacies are constructed is more important today than it has been for many years. In January 2020, unemployment stood at

Introduction

4 per cent, the lowest rate since 1974, yet this masks a workforce forced to contend with increasingly precarious working conditions, zero-hour contracts and wages that are stagnating or actively declining, in real terms. The miners' strikes of the 1970s and 1980s and the declining influence of the union movement that followed the defeat of the 1984–5 strike has left the UK in a position in which labour representation is at one of its lowest ever levels.[1]

This book considers the representation of strike narratives in the work of six contemporary poets. It examines how these poets contend with the declining influence of trade unions in the UK, and how they confront and question the continuing (and contested) legacies that have been produced by, and in response to, industrial disputes of the 1970s and 1980s. Their poems are spaces where the social narratives around labour histories can be interrogated, retold and re-formed.

*

In June 2018, Glen Jacques, a receptionist at the University of London and member of the Independent Workers Union of Great Britain (IWGB), wrote a letter to the Vice-Chancellor of the University of London, Adrian Smith. Jacques wrote that when he took up the role years before, he 'was so proud to get a job working for a prestigious university with a good reputation, very good working conditions and a very good pension'. He had planned for the job to see him through until retirement (@IWGBUniversityLondon). Within two years, he was told that his job would be outsourced to a contract company. He could accept the move or he would be made redundant but, either way, it meant the loss of his pension. Over the next 12 years, who 'owned' his employment changed hands on three more occasions. Jacques wrote, in response to his treatment and many others', that 'every pyramid is only as strong as its foundation, and if the foundation is not maintained to a high standard, the pyramid will, in time, collapse' (@IWGBUniversityLondon 2018). The workers are this foundation, a foundation upon which our societies are built. It is trade unions that have long been instrumental in the provision and implementation of workers' rights and responsible for the improvement of labour

---

[1] Between 1985 and 2016, the number of union members dropped from 10.82 million to 6.86 million. While the number of workers on zero-hour contracts fluctuated from 100,000 to 200,000 between 2000 to 2010, between 2011 and 2016 it rocketed to over 900,000 (Petkova 2018, 4–5). Around 6 per cent of contracts in the UK have no guaranteed number of hours (NGHC) and '28% of businesses with employment of 250 and over make some use of NGHCs, compared with 5% of businesses with employment of less than 10' (Petkova 2018, 6).

conditions. A recent study published by the Institute for Public Policy Research (IPPR) found that

> [a]s union membership increased in the last century, there was a significant fall in inequality. However, as membership has declined since 1979, so inequality has risen to levels not seen for nearly a century. Additionally, countries that have higher rates of collective bargaining have lower levels of inequality; and within firms where there is a trade union present, pay inequality is less.
> (Institute for Public Policy Research 2018)

Trade unions matter. The decline in trade union membership in the UK is a problem. It is a problem tied to the narratives and stories that are told in regard to what a trade union is, what they do and the role they have played and continue to play in contemporary British politics.

According to the most recent statistics, in the UK around 6.44 million people in employment are members of a trade union, which accounts for 23.1 per cent of workers. Comparing this with the peak of UK trade unionism in 1979, when 13.2 million people were members of a union, from a significantly smaller population base, it is not difficult to argue that in real terms the trade union movement's influence and reach is in decline.[2] A combination of restrictive legislation and public disenchantment has led to a position where 'after three decades of persecution, unions are no longer part of the workplace culture' (Jones 2012, 49).[3] While Owen Jones's point rings true for a private sector in which only 12.8 per cent of employees are union members, in the public sector trade union density is a much more robust, if much reduced, 50.1 per cent (Department for Business, Energy and Industrial Strategy 2022, 7). Supermarket union representative Mary Cunningham, interviewed by Owen Jones for his book *Chavs: The Demonization of the Working Class*, provides the depressing summation that, simply, 'a lot of people these days don't even know what a union is about' (2012, 155). Micah Uetricht echoes this sentiment, albeit in an American context, in his book on the Chicago teachers' strike of 2012: 'to many it is a wonder [unions] have not gone extinct' (2014, 114).

---

[2] It should be made clear that the figures here are for those currently in work, those for 1979 include all of the population, regardless of employment status.

[3] The 1980 Employment Act, the 1982 Employment Act, the 1984 Employment Act, the 1986 Public Order Act and the Trade Union Act 2016, to name just a few. When the Labour Party came to power in 1997, Tony Blair boasted 'that even after his trade reforms, trade union laws would remain the "most restrictive" in the Western World' (Jones 2012, 49).

Introduction

Yet, as Nick Cohen writes in the *Guardian*, 'we ought to be living in a stirring age of worker resistance' (2018, n.pag.). An article written by Gavin Kelly and Daniel Tomlinson of the Resolution Foundation—a think-tank that researches living standards in the UK—asserts that 'on the face of it you might think that the future is full of potential for trade unions' as 'public concerns over low pay have soared to record levels over recent years. And, after almost disappearing from view, there is an increasingly noisy debate about the quality and dignity of work in today's Britain'. While these claims are unsupported in the article, Kelly and Tomlinson go on to assert that 'four in five people in Great Britain think that trade unions are "essential" to protect workers' interests' (2016, 10). However, as Cohen's 'ought to be' and Kelly and Tomlinson's 'you might think' suggest, union membership is barely increasing. We seem aware of the importance of trade unions, but there is clearly an issue when it comes to securing members.

*

The state's ability to control the 'legal narrative' surrounding trade unions feeds into the legacies that the poems in this work are negotiating. Governmental legislation affects how trade unions are perceived. The legislative history of trade unions is one of suppression and state authority, and one which seeks to portray unions and collective organisation as a threat to the state itself. To understand the position trade unions currently occupy in the UK, and the prevailing public perception of them, it is pertinent to see these narratives as part of a broader struggle between the state and the labouring classes. As far back as 1563, the Statute of Artificers set out 'a regulation of labour, which sought to banish idleness, advance husbandry, and yield "a convenient proportion" of wages' (Hargreaves 2009). In effect, it became a 'criminal offence for a workman to strike [...] if he thereby broke his contract with the employer' (Frow, Frow & Katanka 1971, ix). The Statute would not be repealed until the beginning of the 1800s. Later, the 1799 Combination Act and the 1800 Combination Act further strengthened anti-union legislation by outlawing any and all forms of working-class collective bargaining or organisation. In essence, the Combination Acts made trade unions illegal, even though the legislation already in place had made 'almost any trade union activity liable to prosecution' (Thompson 1968, 550). From the earliest days of trade union legislation, there is an underlying fear of the collective—the fear that workers might organise and use their collective weight to advance their own economic and social causes.

The 1799 and 1800 acts were not repealed until 1824, with the introduction of the Combinations of Workmen Act. Yet, after the repeal led to a wave of unrest and strike action, the 1825 Combinations of Workmen Act was instituted and, once again, severely limited the 'legal' role of unions.

While trade unions were no longer technically illegal, they would not be legalised by Act of Parliament in the UK until the Trade Union Act of 1871.

This is by no means an exhaustive history of trade unionism in the UK. The book from which much of the information in the previous two paragraphs is taken, *Strikes: A Documentary History*, lists 41 strikes of note in the 114-year period between the Cotton Strike in Scotland in 1812 and 1926's General Strike. What lists like these cannot represent is the legacies that these events create and the cultural narratives they form. What this book looks to do is examine the representations of trade unions in six contemporary poets—by 'contemporary' referring to the period 1972 to 2015. The period begins with the 1972 miners' strike and ends with the thirtieth anniversary of the 1984–5 miners' strike. This concentration on trade union action allows an exploration of questions regarding shifting ideas of the collective, the individual and notions of (post-industrial) place. By exploring alternative representations and narratives surrounding strike action and trade unions, I argue for poetry as a form through which dominant narratives and official histories can be contested. This is not to say that all of the poems here offer radical rewritings of trade union narratives, the poems are themselves indebted to the histories and narratives that precede them. These poems are themselves a product of these histories and the broader cultural representations in movies and the arts that have come to inform our own thinking about trade unions and strike action.

The formal possibilities of poetry allow us to address histories in a nonlinear way, or they offer new access to these histories without defaulting to linear, prescribed forms. The space and arrangement of the poem force us to address the constructed nature of our histories. What the poets in this book do, particularly those writing after 2010, is bring influences from other poems, from movies and television and from official narratives on to the page, sometimes brazenly, sometimes obscured, but always with a sense that they are writing out of and into a strike history. For most, the legacy of the miners' strike of 1984–5 is particularly important, be that because these poets lived through the strike itself or grew up in its wake. The poets explored here understand these strike legacies as artful constructions, foregrounding an awareness of our stories and histories as products that have been manufactured and arranged, in the same way that the poems themselves are artfully rendered and established on the page. These poems are a continuation of and comment on the legacy of these narratives and histories.

*

'Narrative' is a phrase that appears often within this book. Narrative acts as a representation of an idea or function that reflects the aims of the whole. Yet, rather than reflect the 'whole', dominant labour narratives reflect the aims of those who would seek to present their representation of labour histories as absolute or beyond dispute. Narrative here has much in common with Raymond Williams's 'hegemony', in that narratives are not simply concerned with 'matters of direct political control' but also come to 'describe a more general predominance which includes, as one of its key features, a particular way of seeing the world and human nature and relationships' (Williams 1989a, 145). Simply put, dominant narratives (constructed by powerful actors and groups) attempt to obscure those narratives and alternative voices that seek to challenge them. Dominant narratives express the needs (and wants) of a dominant class.

In regard to the poems in this work, 'narrative' appears the most fitting term to describe the exploration and questioning of strike histories and union representations that the poems engage in. The poems draw attention to how these narratives are packaged and presented, as well as who controls these representations. When talking about how trade unions are presented in the poems, 'narrative' suggests movement and process, whereas something like 'image' is too static. As Susan Sontag says, albeit in regard to photography, 'a narrative seems likely to be more effective than an image. Partly it is a question of the length of time one is obliged to look, to feel. No photograph or portfolio of photographs can unfold, go further, and further still' (2003, 109). At their best, narratives reveal how representations and attitudes have changed, how they developed and how they have been formed and re-formed. The term 'narrative' works to connect the representations of strike histories and trade unions in the poems with broader conversations around what it means to write labour histories, and the role of trade unions in society. The individual poems do not present static, isolated images, they contribute to alternative labour narratives and challenge those dominant narratives that seek to paint trade unions as, at best, an irrelevance.

I. Why Poetry?

While poetry does not have the commercial or cultural reach of novels or movies, it has an immediacy that allows it to talk directly to political issues and times of social unrest. Poetry is both an occasion and often, in the public sense, occasional.[4]

---

[4] An 'occasional poem' is one 'written to describe or comment on a particular event and often written for a public reading' ('Occasional Poem'). An example would be 'Praise Song for the Day', written by Elizabeth Alexander for the inauguration of Barack Obama's first term as President of the United States. Alexander writes that 'any thing can be made, any sentence begun' (2009, n.pag.). It is written with a public in mind, written to be spoken before an audience has a chance to read

Introduction

Marian Sugano says of occasional poetry, in her book *The Poetics of the Occasion*, that 'the occasional poem would seem in some sense to evidence both poetry's greatest potential and its most inferior productions, its most famous works and its moments least worthy of inscription' (1992, 3). Sugano's point, a development of the one Hegel makes in volume two of *Aesthetics* (1975, 995–6), is that the occasional poem is too indebted, too dependent on the event which inspires its creation and which allows or creates an audience for its reception. The argument is essentially that these poems are too concerned with events of the present: the less current the event within one's (and society's) own cultural memory, the less 'worthy' the poem that represents it. Sugano's point seems to presuppose that occasional poetry must be produced in the immediate wake, or even in advance, of the occasion. The occasional poem can be immediate; however, the gap between the occasion and the poem need not be so brief. In his defence of the poetry of Ben Jonson against the charge of being 'occasional poetry' and the 'trivial or insincere writing' that he sees this phrase as having come to indicate, Thom Gunn writes that:

> [A]ll poetry is occasional: whether the occasion is an external event like a birthday or a declaration of war, whether it is an occasion of the imagination, or whether it is in some sort of combination of the two. (After all, the external may lead to the internal occasions.) The occasion in all cases—literal or imaginary—is the starting point, only, of a poem, but it should be a starting point to which the poet must in some sense stay true. The truer he is to it, the closer he sticks to what for him is its authenticity, the more he will be able to draw from it in the adventures that it produced, adventures that consist of the experience of writing. (1982, 106–7)

it. This type of poem anticipates its own importance. In this case, it is written knowing that the event it is commemorating is already historic. Another type of 'occasional poem' would be 'This Is the Place' by Tony Walsh—also known as 'Longfella'. Written after the 2017 Manchester Arena attack, the poem is an 'ode' to Manchester's history and strength in the face of its present trauma. The day after the attack on 22 May 2017 in which 22 innocent people died, Walsh performed 'This Is the Place' to the thousands of people who had gathered in Manchester's Albert Square for a vigil for those who had lost their lives. Walsh's reading was broadcast around the world, and the poem republished in such places as the *Manchester Evening News*, *The New Statesman* and the *Sun*. This is the occasional poem at its best: harnessing poetry's ability to respond with near immediacy to an event and then be disseminated in such a way as to offer support and an articulation of a social 'feeling' or mood. While this is one way of thinking about poetry, of an immediacy that comes through public readings, we might also consider work that is published after an event, work that is interested in the legacies of an event, as containing elements of the 'occasional'.

Introduction

It is the link that Gunn makes between the 'internal' and the 'external' and their counterpoints in the 'singular' and the 'collective' voice that interests me. If the 'occasion' is only the starting point, then the poem must be (and do) something more, be something else, than a reflection of an occasion. The occasion is generative, up to a point: and that is the point at which the poem is written and itself begins to generate responses to the occasion (through readers' encounters with it). Behind Gunn's notion of the poet staying in some sense true to the occasion lurks the idea of the poem as a form by which to interrogate and reflect, in all senses of the word, the mediation between the singular and collective voice that is at the heart of political and industrial disputes.

To stay true, particularly to a social or political occasion, requires an effort to balance the twin drives of reconciliation and estrangement. This reconciliation and estrangement is performed by the poems and poets in this book through their distance from, and lack of direct involvement in, the events about which they write. While these poets were not involved in these events, they are nonetheless caught up in their legacies. The poet must reconcile their own view of an event (and the 'official' history of it) with cultural products and depictions of the occasion, while simultaneously creating a work that by its very newness brings into question those truths we may have taken to be absolute. The poems in this work may grow out of an occasion, but this is a poetry that allows and foregrounds, through its formal and linguistic stylings, an ability to linger on and contend with the fractures, the complications and the language itself we use to talk about ourselves and our individual and collective histories.

There is something in Gunn's idea that brings to mind the oft-misinterpreted line from W.H. Auden's 'In Memory of W.B. Yeats' that 'poetry makes nothing happen'. Here, the end of the line is frequently overlooked: while 'poetry makes nothing happen: it survives' (1979, 81). The colon between the 'happening' and the 'survival', serves as a gate between the 'original' happening and the legacy of the event in which the poem exists. The stanza ends with a reassertion by Auden: 'it survives, / A way of happening, a mouth' (1979, 81). Auden is not saying that poetry does nothing, but that poetry is itself a happening, that it is a space and a vehicle for alternative voices to be heard and narratives to be expressed.

More contemporaneously, A.F. Moritz, in his 2009 Wordsworth-invoking essay 'What Man Has Made of Man: Can Poetry Reconnect the Individual and Society?', sees contemporary poetry as 'bound up with the problem of isolation and communion' and this as being 'our basic social question' (2009, n.pag.). Moritz's belief is that 'poetry is inward self-development *plus* the insistence that this must have a principal place in the public forum *plus* a third thing, a conclusion that flows from the first two' (2009, n.pag.). It is this 'conclusion', one which doesn't necessarily 'flow' from the first two things, but is almost riven from them, while trying simultaneously to knit them together, that is explored in the poems that follow: the negotiation of the singular and the collective, the 'me/us' and the 'you/them', the public and the private, the trade union and the worker, the interior and the exterior. How is it that these things come to shape and be shaped by our strike narratives and legacies?

By looking at the poetry of Barry MacSweeney, Tony Harrison, Sean O'Brien—focusing predominantly on works authored between the middle of the 1970s and the mid-to-late 1980s—and the post-2010 poetry by Helen Mort, Steve Ely and Paul Bentley, it is possible to argue for the ways in which their works give a different account of the marginalisation of trade unions within contemporary political structures. Undoubtedly, the 1984–5 strike occupies much of the thinking in this book and the thinking of the poets focused on. However, the intention was always to talk about strike action and trade unions more broadly, even if, unsurprisingly, much of the poetry written regarding unions comes out of or as a response to industrial action.

II. Introducing the Poets

Barry MacSweeney, Tony Harrison and Sean O'Brien are in some ways the 'foundation' upon which this work is built. They are the writers who confront issues regarding labour representation and strike action. Their responses, while not always immediate, come from a place of experience, the experience of those living, and having lived, through the strikes of the 1970s and 1980s. They are three poets whose engagement with the disputes and issues this work focuses on is pronounced.

Starting with Barry MacSweeney (1948–2000). In a note written in 1967 and published in the short-lived magazine *The English Intelligencer*,[5] MacSweeney called for a form of poetry union, or at least an organisation of sorts, with, as Luke Roberts puts it, 'some unexpected additions' (2017, 53):

> a Writers Union! Its [*sic*] that ballpoint and bayonet again. for something dear to me [...] I feel closer to Russian poets than any others in the history of the world. Tribunes, that's them. Unionists in verse! Strikers with poems. I need to be a tribune. (MacSweeney 2014, 145)[6]

---

[5] MacSweeney was later to be heavily involved with the National Union of Journalists (NUJ) while working for the *Kentish Times*.
[6] The model that MacSweeney was looking to was Vladimir Mayakovsky's Federation of Soviet Writers, whose first official meeting took place in 1926. Poet Bob Cobbing, a friend of MacSweeney, attempted to establish a similar union for poets in the UK, Poets Conference. While the name 'Poets Union'

Introduction

In MacSweeney's *Wolf Tongue: Selected Poems 1965–2000* more than half of the book focuses on poems after 1990.[7] Much of the focus on MacSweeney here comes through the poem 'Black Torch Sunrise', although Chapter Three looks to 1997's 'John Bunyan to Johnny Rotten', in order to examine MacSweeney's treatment of Thatcher and Scargill. Written in the aftermath of the 1972 and 1974 miners' strikes, 'Black Torch Sunrise' is the only poem from 1978's *Black Torch* that MacSweeney chose for inclusion in his *Selected Poems*. In 'Black Torch Sunrise' MacSweeney writes that 'facts revealed / must be published / because they are seditious' (1978, 71). Chapter Two takes its lead from MacSweeney's reference to the TUC (Trades Union Congress) in this poem and its link to state power. In a preface to *Black Torch*, published in *Bezoar*, MacSweeney makes it clear that the starting point and inspiration for the work is the 1844 Durham miners' strike. For MacSweeney, that strike was a turning point, and an event whose legacy he saw in the industrial disputes of the early 1970s:

> It laid a tough foundation which still makes the National Union of Mineworkers the strongest most radical union in the land. Ask Edward Heath. They toppled his Tory Government in May, 1973. (MacSweeney in Roberts 2017, 62)

While almost 40,000 people went on strike during the 1844 dispute, it would end in defeat for the miners. The end of the strike came when the mine owners imported workers from Ireland and rural Wales, both places chosen because of their lack of an organised labour movement (Engels 2009, 257). As MacSweeney writes in the poem 'Black Torch':

> stoppage is almost total
> the union is the most effective
> ever seen
> in the two counties. (1978, 15)

The way to undermine an effective strike is to undermine the union. According to MacSweeney, it is not enough that the strikers or miners are 'effective', the union itself must also be effective. The 'union' is the workers and their representatives both working towards the same end. The

---

was originally mooted, some poets did not want the word 'union' associated with their organisation. Stephen Willey argues that 'the unease that some of Cobbing's contemporaries felt about the word "union" reveals their deeper discomfort about aligning the writing of poetry with struggles in other labour markets' (2012, 254). Barry MacSweeney did not harbour any such unease.

[7] The poems in the book were based on selections made by MacSweeney in 1999.

'stoppage' rests on the union. Yet, as Luke Roberts says in reference to the period during which *Black Torch* was written and published,

> [w]here Black Torch had begun in the triumphant afterglow of the successful National Union of Mineworkers (NUM) strikes in 1972 and 1974, it ended with the collapse and betrayal of the trade union movement, paving the way for Thatcherism. (2017, 74)

MacSweeney is a poet who, for all his involvement with the union movement and his clear belief in the power and necessity of trade unionism, clearly holds reservations regarding parts of the union movement and those steering the future of trade unionism.

Unlike MacSweeney, Tony Harrison's inclusion is no surprise in a work about poetry and labour disputes. Harrison's poem 'V.' (1985) is arguably the best-known of his poetic works. And, following its broadcast on Channel 4 in 1987, it is surely the only poem to find itself subject to debate in the House of Commons Early Day Motion under the banner of television obscenity.[8] While the broadcast of the poem came only a few years after the 1984–5 miners' strike, when it was still a sensitive issue politically and socially, the Commons Motion was purely concerned with the 'obscenities' that threaten 'broadcasting standards' ('No. 31 Notices of Motions: 27th October 1987' in Harrison 2008, 60). There are dozens of expletives in the poem, and the *Daily Mail* noted that 'the crudest, most offensive word is used 17 times' ('Four-Letter TV Poem Fury' in Harrison 2008, 40).

Fear of obscenity aside, the poem itself was written in a 'vandalised cemetery in Leeds during the Miners' Strike' (Astley 2008, 35). Terry Eagleton comments in his review of the poem that 'the actual Miners' Strike impinges on **v.** [*sic*] hardly at all, other than in a moving epigraph taken from Arthur Scargill' (1991, 350). However, an epigraph from Scargill, a figure

---

[8] The actual motion tabled by MP Gerald Howarth, now Sir Gerald and Conservative Party MP until 2017, reads: 'This House is appalled at plans by Channel 4 to screen with the approval of the Independent Broadcasting Authority the poem 'V.' by Tony Harrison; whilst recognising that the poem may not be wholly devoid of literary merit, considers that the stream of obscenities contained in the poem is profoundly offensive and will serve to hasten the decline of broadcasting standards' ('No. 31 Notices of Motions: 27th October 1987' in Harrison 2008, 60). Norman Buchan, a Labour MP for Paisley South at the time, had some suggested amendments to make to the motion: 'Line 1, leave out "at" to end and add "the apparent failure of certain honourable Members to have read the poem V or, if they read it, to have understood it; points out that the whole purpose of the poem is to emphasise the real offensiveness of the obscenities referred to"' (No. 31 Notices of Motions: 27th October 1987 in Harrison 2008, 60).

Introduction

who could in no way be considered politically neutral, invokes issues of class and power and, as a corollary, workers' movements and unionisation more broadly. Indeed, as Harrison notes in his lecture 'The Inky Digit of Defiance', given at the ceremony for the inaugural PEN Pinter Prize in 2009, 'what aggravated many even more than the language was that they thought I had dedicated the poem to Arthur Scargill, the leader of the miners' union' (2017, 458). The simple inclusion of Scargill, particularly as the work's opening gambit, means that 'V.' is wedded to the miners' strike of 1984–5 and the trade union movement that Scargill had come to represent.

The issues surrounding class and industrial decline that 'V.' interrogates have been found throughout Harrison's work. On stage, Harrison's adaptations of the medieval mystery plays *The Nativity*, *The Passion* and *Doomsday* have biblical figures in the uniforms of miners, painters, butchers, ticket conductors and others. *Doomsday* opens with God illuminating the head of Jesus with a miner's lamp and stating, with a nod to the labouring classes and more specifically miners, that 'to hell now will I fare / To claim back what is mine' (Harrison 1999, 162). The play, about God's disillusionment with man, has the miners' lamps searching for an entrance into hell, as a symbol of miners' descent into the dark of the pits, but also as a comment on the decline of the mining industry in the north-east, where over one hundred pits had been closed between 1950 and 1970. First staged in 1977, the plays—perhaps coincidentally—really came to public attention in 1985, when *Doomsday* was nominated for Best New Play at the Olivier Awards.

As far back as 1974's 'Them and [uz]', Harrison's work has struggled against a conception of poetry that is purely there to glorify, or represent and speak to, an elite. In the poem, a teacher opines in relation to Harrison's northern accent and reading of Macbeth that 'Poetry's the speech of kings. You're one of those / Shakespeare gives the comic bits to: prose!' (1995, 33). Harrison writes in the opening lines to the poem's second section: 'So right, yer buggers, then! We'll occupy / your lousy leasehold Poetry' (1995, 34). Harrison's occupation is the language of struggle, the 'them' and 'us' and the language of taking control and establishing a place for oneself. Yet, particularly in 'V.', Harrison foregrounds and interrogates easy (and lazy) categorisation, while drawing attention to the relatively privileged position that is required to make art in the first instance:

> *Aspirations, cunt! Folk on t' fucking dole*
> *'ave got about as much scope to aspire*
> *above the shit they're dumped in, cunt, as coal*
> *aspires to be chucked on t' fucking fire.* (2008, 17)

'Aspirations' are tied up with economic security and freedoms. By aligning those on the 'dole' with 'coal', Harrison suggests that without work you lose political and social agency, you become nothing more than an object to be 'chucked on t'fucking fire'. Sean O'Brien claims that what most concerns Harrison is the power that language 'confers and the restraints under which some of its users labour' (2012, 33). Harrison's work is about the ways in which language can be wielded, and the politics surrounding who is included or excluded from this.

Although he is a pre-eminent critic of Harrison and contemporary poetry more generally, Sean O'Brien's inclusion is for his poetry. W.N. Herbert and Matthew Hollis write that O'Brien's work 'often reflects the fierce regional inequalities stoked-up under Thatcherism' (2000, 296). These regional inequalities point towards the widening, both culturally and economically, of the north-south divide, the decline of industry in the north and the rise of the financial and service sectors in London and the south. This concern with the insidious effects of Thatcherism extends throughout O'Brien's work, from his first collection, *The Indoor Park* (1983), in which he writes, in 'The Park by the Railway', of 'Coal and politics, invisible decades / Of rain, domestic love and failing mills / That ended in a war and then a war' (2012, 11), all the way to his 2015 collection, *The Beautiful Librarians*, where he reminisces about a time in which 'someone stole the staffroom tin / Where we collected for the miners, for the strike they couldn't win' (6).[9] These poems highlight the concern with politics, and more specifically Thatcherism and union action, that often characterises O'Brien's poetry. These selections from two works published over thirty years apart show a writer engaged with questions regarding the legacies of industrial action in their poetry.

In 'Another Country', O'Brien writes of the legacy of the miners' strike of 1984–5 that: 'Where all year long the battle raged, there's "landscape" and a plaque, / But though you bury stuff forever, it keeps on coming back' (2015, 7). The poem brings into a shared space the image of the plaque and that of an industrial landscape. O'Brien puts them in conversation with one another, demonstrating the ways in which our histories come to be managed. Yet this management is not absolute. The starting point is not simply in a slavish response to the events and the political attitudes themselves, but in poetry as a generative form, as a way of creating something new, of adding a new voice or dimension to a narrative and as a way of considering the responses to politics and political elites. This is an idea of a poetry that is both intrinsically public and political. In an interview he gave to Andrew

---

[9] O'Brien has spoken about this event in an interview with Andrew McAllister printed in the short-lived poetry magazine *Bete Noire*: 'We ran a collection for the NUM. Somebody stole it. I don't know who. It didn't raise that much money […] being the kind of place that it was' (O'Brien quoted in Woodcock 1998, 55). This 'kind of place' was the Sussex comprehensive school he was working in at the time.

Introduction

Mitchell in 1992, O'Brien sets out his view on the interplay between the private and the public:

> the effort of the poem is to see the process as a whole, to see it entire; not to say 'There's politics and here is the private life', but to suggest that the two are inextricably bound up with each other, that they are really metaphors of each other. (O'Brien quoted in Woodcock 1998, 38)

The 'effort' that O'Brien speaks of situates poetry as itself a form of labour power. O'Brien points to a politics in his poetry, and perhaps 'political poetry' more generally, that acts as representation, helping to reveal forms of (seemingly disparate) lived experience. Woodcock sees in O'Brien's work a poetry that is 'concerned with rendering the concrete experiences which the imagination offers in such a way as to reveal that complex process at work, and hence display the interconnections between the seemingly different categories or areas of human experience' (1999, 38). O'Brien's poetry can perform these complexities, bringing to the page disparate forms of experience presented as a unified, but not uniform, representation.

*

This book in large part focuses on the periods 1976–88 and 2010–15 quite simply because poetry that concerns itself with trade union issues appears and reappears at these times. The first period traces the end of the 1972 and 1974 miners' strikes through to the immediate aftermath of the 1984–5 miners' strike. After 2010, a number of newer poets (particularly from the north-east) appeared, most of them publishing their first collections or pamphlets, whose work starts to engage with union action and industrial disputes, particularly with regards to the 1984–5 miners' strike and its twenty-fifth and thirtieth anniversaries.

The year 2011 saw the publication of Paul Bentley's pamphlet *Largo*, which includes 'The Two Magicians'. The poem, which draws heavily on Bentley's experiences of growing up in Yorkshire during the 1984–5 strike, is cut through with references to literature and pop culture, and underpinned by lengthy quotations taken from the oral history *Thurcroft: A Village and the Miners' Strike*. One stanza in 'The Two Magicians' opens with the lines: 'Into the blue unclouded weather. / *It were like a holiday.* / Trailing my shadow the other way. / My Morrissey melancholy' (Bentley 2011, 19). Bentley presents a line from Tennyson's 'The Lady of Shalott', before moving to the words of a miner, a repurposed line from Proust and, finally, a reference to the singer from the band The Smiths. It is the splicing together of these layers of cultural awareness that, as Matthew Stewart suggests in his review of the pamphlet, portrays 'a voice that wants to belong in spite of the separating force of its load of acquired knowledge' while at the same time juxtaposing and intermingling 'higher and lower linguistic register[s]' in its portrayal of the strike (2012, n.pag.). The poem questions how our narratives come to be formed, who speaks them (and is able to) and the ways in which our cultural pasts come to influence and shape the present.

Helen Mort's debut collection, *Division Street* (2013), in its cover art (a photograph by Don McPhee of a striking miner confronting a police officer) and its central and longest poem, 'Scab', puts striking front and centre. Of 'Scab' Mort has said that:

> I felt a great urge to write it because my generation grew up with the legacy of the miners' strike and Thatcherism, which marked both the landscape and the lives of everyone in the area in one way or another. We need to keep the memory of that time alive. Orgreave and the strike were about divisions in society, not just among the miners. (2016)

What is clear from Mort's comments is that her work is contending with legacies—legacies into which she was born, in 1985. Mort is very much a child of the strike. In 'Scab', her engagement is with the aftermath of the 1984–5 miners' strike and what it means to write histories of political and social upheaval, the need to keep memories 'of that time alive' and how it is that we come to construct those memories in a 'landscape' marked by the after effects of Thatcherism in the UK. Yet, in an interview she gave to *Granta*, Mort talks of how she felt, in regard to being 'hardly born at the time of the strike', that in some ways she 'wasn't qualified to say anything about' the dispute (Mort & Allen 2013). Here Mort reveals something that this work considers, not just regarding what stories we tell, but who tells, and who feels able to tell, our stories to and for us.

The final poet of this triumvirate is Steve Ely and his first two published collections, *Oswald's Book of Hours* (2013) and *Englaland* (2015). *Englaland* opens with an epigraph from William Faulkner's *Requiem for a Nun* that appears to underpin much of Ely's work: 'The past is never dead. It's not even past' (2015, n.pag.). For Ely the past is part of our present. It is a present in which the past exists as an actor in poems (and playlets) that have the Duke of Wellington at war against Peter Mandelson and Arthur Scargill rubbing shoulders with ex-British National Party leader Nick Griffin. Ely has said that 'behind both *Oswald's Book of Hours* and *Englaland* is a vision of England in which fifteen hundred years of history, culture and language exist simultaneously as an irreducible synoptic unity' (Ely & Pugh 2015). The past lives with us, it is an active part of the present. It is simply part of the thing itself, incapable of division. Or as Sheenagh Pugh puts it 'the past is not past: it is in the present and intrinsic to it; it is how the present came to be' (Ely & Pugh 2015).

Ely claims now to be 'politically quiescent' on the grounds that, since renouncing political party membership in 1996, he doesn't 'count simply "having opinions", even on social media (or in poems), as being politically engaged'. He says that one has 'to join, campaign, organise, commit, sacrifice' in order to be politically active (Ely & Pugh 2015).[10] While Ely suggests that the writing of poems doesn't mean one is politically engaged or active, that does not exclude the poems themselves from being politically motivated. Ely's work is unquestionably political and frequently trade union-focused. Where most of the other poets in this book, bar MacSweeney, narrow their union focus to the strike of 1984–5, Ely's poetry ranges far more widely 'with an imperative sense that this England is continuously one language, one people, and one landscape' (Brown 2016, n.pag.). *Oswald's* includes the poem 'Arthur Scargill', which credits Scargill with a range of achievements including providing miners with 'health and Palma de Mallorca' (Ely 2013, 71). Ely's second collection, *Englaland*, continues in a similar vein to *Oswald's* with numerous references to Arthur Scargill and the National Union of Mineworkers (NUM), along with namechecking the Union of Democratic Mineworkers (UDM), the Trades Union Congress (TUC) and the Union of Construction, Allied Trades and Technicians (UCATT). In Ely's 'England'—his poetic conception of England being very much a northern, male one—trade unions are a part of the language, people and landscape and 'how the present came to be'.

While women make up just under 57 per cent of trade union members in the UK (Department for Business, Energy and Industrial Strategy 2022, 8),[11] Ely's 'male' conception of a strike history is not an unusual position, at least in terms of British poets. It is clearly not that women have played no role in contemporary strike histories. In the UK, there was the 1968 Ford Sewing Machinists' Strike that led to the Equal Pay Act 1970 and the Grunwick strike in 1976, to name two. Internationally,

---

[10] Ely expanded on his political 'history' in an interview in 2012: 'I'm a former socialist—I was in and around the left for large parts of the early eighties and early nineties (with an interlude in the Green Party) and I retain some of the atavisms of the left, such as a knee jerk animus to Conservatism [...] But I haven't been a member of a political party since 1996 and my political activism since then has been non-existent'.

[11] In 2021, 30.3 per cent of Black or Black British female employees were trade union members, as were 26.6 per cent of white female employees, 23.1 per cent of female employees who identified as mixed ethnicity, 23.1 per cent of Asian or Asian British female employees and 16.1 per cent of Chinese female employees or those from another ethnic group (Department for Business, Energy and Industrial Strategy 2022).

there was Women Strike for Peace in 1961 and the Women's Strike for Equality in 1970 and, more recently, the International Women's Strikes of 2017 and 2018. Carol Stephenson and Jean Spence claim, in relation to the 1984–5 miners' strike, that 'female strike activism not only challenged popular preconceptions about the conservatism of working-class women, but also extended the reach of the strike beyond the traditional frontiers of industrial disputes' (2012, 2). Yet none of these narratives and challenges to preconceptions seem to find their way into contemporary British poetry. At the more extreme end of this, Carolyn Forché says in her introduction to an anthology of twentieth-century poetry of witness that, in terms of her selections, 'fewer women poets seem to have survived the horrors of our century than their male counterparts, and many fewer have been translated' (1993, 31). This survival is obviously not the case with the miners' strike, nor is the question of translation. However, it does speak to a potential reason for the relative silence of women poets writing about strike action. Fewer women's stories of strike action in Britain seem to have survived. Katy Shaw, in *Mining the Meaning*, examines poems written by those 'whose actions authored the conflict' of the 1984–5 miners' strike—strikers and their families, particularly women—and how these voices have been negated. This 'strike literature', as Shaw terms it, and the attention given to it, has been neglected. For women, and poems written by them, this situation is even more pronounced. In *Mining the Meaning*, there are poems found written on scraps of paper and cereal packets (2012, 1). They are not part of mainstream poetry publishing, or publishing at all. These stories have to be found, to be searched for.

The history, or at least narrative, of trade unions in the UK is for the most part a white, male working-class one. The stories told of strike activism are in general of men striking, of men picketing. We see so little of women in these stories. This is a choice that says that the act of men striking is interesting, not women on strike, or the fundraising, or the creation and management of domestic spaces, or their 'independent strike activism' (Stephenson & Spence 2012, 8), essentially anything away from the picket line—particularly here in regard to the miners' strikes that provide a large part of this book's content. Helen Mort writes about the town in which she grew up, but the strike history is of scabs and re-enactments of the Battle of Orgreave, all male spaces. Bentley's work, coming from his own experience of growing up during the strike, does look towards a world where women join pickets and occupy domestic spaces, yet with the goal of supporting their husbands and, frequently, children. There is the sense that women's activism was 'other-centred' (Stephenson & Spence 2012, 8). In these poems, and in strike histories of the UK more generally, this has led to women playing, or being relegated to, a supporting role at best.

What the poets in this book seem to be writing against is an official strike narrative that paints (predominantly) male strikers as an enemy.

Introduction

Perhaps this is part of the reason why there are fewer women poets writing about strike action and female strike activism; their stories are not the ones that dominate, not the ones that are at the forefront of the narrative, not the ones that feel like they 'need' to be defended or corrected. The earlier poets in this work, MacSweeney, Harrison and O'Brien, write to correct the story of those who were striking; the later poets write to update and contend with a legacy informed by those earlier stories. Alan Sinfield claims that it is 'the contest between rival stories [that] produces our notions of reality' (2007, 26–7). In these poetic strike narratives, with no contest to speak of, this 'reality' is one that neglects the stories of women, and those written by women. Stephenson and Spence say that there is a question to be asked around the extent to which 'women's activism was other-centred and the degree to which they remained rooted in secondary and dependent subject positions despite their independent strike activism' (2012, 8). The idea that women's activism is 'rooted in secondary and dependent subject positions' is fundamental to the problem of why there are so few women poets writing about strike action and activism. The strike stories of women are (and have been) decentred. Men and male poets simply do not have to contend with or fight against this dependent position.

Across all the poets, the only woman we see in most of these strike narratives is Margaret Thatcher. Within these miners' strike histories, and the working-class struggle more broadly, she is the 'enemy', both as herself and as a totemic figure of the Conservative Party and Tory state. Men can be complex or 'good' or 'evil' or somewhere in between, whereas there are no 'women'. What is left in these poems is not a representation of women but of one woman, Thatcher, and a way of writing and talking about her that is almost wholly negative. In Ely's 'Nithing', we have a Thatcher who

> [...] seems to be a woman
> And yet
> An eelpout coils
> In a slimy gusset. (2015, 124)

Thatcher is barely a woman, and depicted with all humanity removed. Not all of Ely's depictions of men, barring Arthur Scargill, are positive; however, in Ely's strike poems, Thatcher is the only woman, and that woman is monstrous.

As James Bloodworth writes in *Hired: Six Months Undercover in Low-Wage Britain*, 'the most important trade union work is typically quite dull'; it is bureaucratic and is concerned with the minutiae of people's jobs and working conditions (2018, 130). Conversely, strikes and the act of striking provide a focal point, something that has narrative potential. Women are often sidelined from these stories. They are (indirectly) told that their work, their role, their labour does not have enough narrative potential to make them the centre of a story. Women poets are not writing about these strikes because they don't see themselves. Women's stories have been ignored by a belief that the images, the narratives that are important are of men picketing, fighting for their way of life and their communities, and of scabs and running battles with the police and the state.

The voice of the working classes has been systematically silenced or sidelined in traditional labour histories. There has been an attempt in official narratives to paint unions as an irrelevance, as a danger to democracy, and to diminish the impact they have had on labour politics in the UK, to erase unions from the grand narrative of the struggle of the working classes. Much of the poetry in this book addresses this first level of 'erasure', that of strike action being for positive social change, against a state intent on eradicating unions and a way of life. In an attempt to restore these stories, what we have are tales and histories of strikes and of workers picketing against big business and the state. These workers are, on the whole, men. In many of the narratives in which women appear, they are there as 'support' to other people's strike stories. The stories of women, and by women, are buried beneath another layer of effacement. While poetry can and does give voice to those sidelined by dominant narratives, it can still only do so if those silenced narratives are seen as having a place, as having something to contribute. The stories of women and strike activism are being ignored. This is why there are so few women poets writing about the miners' strike in particular. The poems and writing by female strike activists that, for example, Stephenson and Spence's work looks to, often write as 'other' in a way which typifies 'the extent to which their struggle and their own identities were invested outside themselves' (2012, 8).

*

Peter Riley has said that it is *'always* worrying when poets get involved in politics', yet perhaps that depends on how we understand 'involved' (2015). The poets in this work are writing about legacies, structures of power and questions of place *through* poetic engagement with trade union representations and strike narratives. What all these poets and their works have in common is that they see poetry as having a role to play in telling these stories, examining these issues and exploring these histories

These poets and their poems are placed in conversation with one another, thematically, to see how they speak across and against one another—how some poems speak louder than others, how some poems turn themselves inwards and others open themselves out. This book does not take a chronological or author-led approach to the subject. The poems do not, for the most part, recount a linear history of responses to an event—this linear history is covered in Chapter One and the post-war history of trade unionism in the UK. What is of interest is where these poems 'overlap',

Introduction

where they rub against each other, and what is created by these tensions and also the gaps that they fill, draw attention to or create in their wake.

III. The Chapters

Chapter One recounts the post-war trade union history of the UK. This brief history serves to contextualise the industrial disputes and political landscape about which these poets are writing, and the limitations of taking a more traditionally historic or quantitative approach to cultural legacies. Chapter Two begins by looking at explicit references to trade unions in the poets' work to assess what it means to talk of trade unions as a collective and how this presents a form of unifying 'voice' able to speak to structures of power. It argues that these representations have the potential to reduce the individual members who make up unions to a homogeneous whole, removing part of their agency as members. The latter part of the chapter focuses on the work of Helen Mort to consider what it means to exclude representations of trade unions from poems that are explicitly concerned with industrial disputes. The work explores how Mort's poem 'Scab' shifts focus away from unions, in an examination of the ways in which certain alternative voices become excluded from 'mainstream' narratives and legacies. Chapter Three turns from considering ideas regarding collectives to those of the individual, with particular attention paid to the two most recognisable and divisive figures of the miners' strike of 1984–5, Arthur Scargill and Margaret Thatcher. Through a consideration of the politics of naming, the chapter explores the ways in which Scargill and Thatcher are 'constructed' through various acts of naming in the poems. It is argued that these acts reveal the means by which various actors attempt to institute forms of cultural dominion and/or opposition in regard to British labour politics and trade unions. Chapter Four is more explicitly about legacies. The chapter takes the three more recent poets and their engagement with the north-east as a starting point to discuss the ways in which legacies—specifically regarding industrial action and trade unions—are liable to co-optation and appropriation by those from outside of these communities. The chapter closes with a discussion of a number of industrial decline movies that are referenced in the poems to probe how these cultural products and the ways in which they retell and repackage these strike narratives can come to obscure the sources from which they originate. Chapter Five begins by considering *Against all the Odds*, a poetry anthology published by the NUM during the 1984–5 strike, to examine what it means to write poetry that is in the process of attempting to establish its own narrative, counter to 'official' narratives. The chapter continues by discussing the role of the poet laureate, with particular attention paid to Ted Hughes, who held the position for the majority of the '84–5 strike, to appraise the 'official' poetic responses to the strike and the space that the poets I focus on seem to be occupying.

The book as a whole seeks not only to address representations of strike action in contemporary English poetry, considering how it is that poets have come to contend with and contribute to presentations and narratives surrounding trade unions and industrial disputes, but to put these representations into conversation with one another. Through these conversations, the work questions the ways in which labour narratives and legacies are constructed and investigates the power dynamics that underpin the (re)presentations of our histories (and the way they are presented to us) with specific focus on what it means to tell the narratives of our strike histories.

CHAPTER ONE

How Did We Get Here? The History

> The most important trade union work is typically quite dull. The best trade union leaders are also, by extension, interested in the boring stuff – the length of the toilet breaks, the rules governing agency workers, the quantity of the paid breaks a worker is entitled to, and so on and so forth. These are the things that matter when you work in a job at the bottom end of the labour market, not the rigid dogmas and slogans summoning a radiant utopian future, nor a new set of superiors booming at you in impenetrable jargon.
> James Bloodworth, *Hired: Six Months Undercover in Low-Wage Britain* (2018)

Tracing the major union events of the twentieth and twenty-first centuries, and the political landscape that underpins them, provides valuable context by which to better explore the work of the contemporary poets in this book. Once the timeline is established, the ways in which the poems seek to complicate pre-existing labour narratives become more explicit. It would seem that any conversation regarding the role of unions in political culture inevitably leads itself through a history of strikes, a history of unionism that has an impact on the public or, at least, a public face.

The story of strikes in the UK in the twentieth century inevitably involves, and here starts from, miners. Within the political and economic history of Britain in the twentieth century, the importance of miners cannot be overstated; Britain, quite simply, 'needed coal, and had needed it for more than a century' (Beckett & Hencke 2009, 2). In 1920, coal accounted for 99 per cent of Britain's fuel input for electricity generation and remained at over 50 per cent—except during the Miners' Strike of 1984, when it dropped to around 45 per cent—until 1995 (Department of Energy and Climate Change 2013). In 1920, with a population of 44 million, over a million people were employed as coal miners in the UK (Department of Energy & Climate Change 2013). In 1920, over 8.3 million people were part of a trade union—45 per cent of the workforce—and yet 'even the biggest general unions were dwarfed by the 900,000-strong Miners' Federation of Great Britain (MFGB)—the aristocracy of organized labour' (Beckett & Hencke 2009, 1–2).

The country's reliance on coal, the sheer number of unionised miners and the solidarity of the workers meant that throughout the twentieth century miners were 'the vanguard of the union movement in Britain', with Britain's only general strike being called in support of them in 1926 (Jones 2012, 55).

On 3 March 1926, the Trades Union Congress called for a sympathetic strike in defence of miners' wages, which were to be cut when government subsidy for the industry expired in May 1926.[1] Yet it was also the TUC who by day eight (of the nine-day strike) were continuing in a 'feverish desire to lift the General Strike without securing protection for the miners' (Cook quoted in Frow, Frow & Katanka 1971, 186). By 12 May, the strike was over: it was a demonstration of the ability of the working classes to organise, and a display of worker solidarity, but it was a show that ended in defeat. Walter Citrine, General Secretary of the TUC from 1926 to 1946, who led the TUC in calling off the strike, claimed that 'the outstanding lesson of the general strike of 1926 is that authority must be invested exclusively and entirely in the directing body' (Citrine, qtd. in Taylor 2000, 36). Citrine was wrong. The outstanding lesson was that a cohesive union movement is more effective than a fractured one. This idea of 'fracturing' appears through Barry MacSweeney's 'Black Torch Sunrise' and Steve Ely's 'Ballad of the Scabs', where the workers strike 'to the silence of the TUC' (Ely 2015, 139). 'Fracturing' works as a way to think about the poems more broadly, the line breaks of the poems helping to articulate the fragmentation that we see in some of these narratives.

The 'standard' history of trade unions in the UK is generally quiet on the period 1926–72, with industrial action during the Second World War often being glossed over.[2] Trade unions did not disappear during wartime. While days lost to strike action during the war were significantly lower than the 126 million of 1926, they were still at their highest in almost a decade in

---

[1] A 'sympathetic' or 'sympathy' strike is one in which workers do not go on strike at their own workplaces, but strike to support other groups of workers on strike. In 1927, as a direct result of the General Strike, the Conservative government passed the Trade Disputes and Trade Unions Act which outlawed the type of sympathy strike seen during the 1926 dispute.

[2] The Office for National Statistics website 'The History of Strikes in the UK' (2015) includes no information on any dispute between 1926's General Strike and 1972's miners' strike.

1944, with 3.7 million days lost ('Labour Disputes' 2018). These wartime figures should be compared with those for 2016, where the UK saw 322,000 days lost due to labour disputes, and those for 2015 with 170,000, the fewest working days lost since the ONS started compiling data. Tony Dabb, in an article in *The Socialist Review*, 'World War 2: Official Secrets', writes of engineering apprentices from Clydesdale, then Coventry, Lancashire and London striking in 1941 over pay issues. The apprentices from Coventry even took the significant step of including women from the local munitions factory, marking a departure 'from the attitude that the influx of women was actually making things worse for men at work' (Dabb 1995, n.pag.). In 1943, there were strikes at the Neptune ship repair yard in Tyneside after five workers refused to join the union, and a major engineering strike at the Vickers-Armstrong yard in Barrow over a basic rate of pay that had not increased in 29 years. In 1944, with the government in desperate need of coal to aid the war effort, the government demanded an increase in coal production, 'yet these extra demands were not received warmly by the miners when their demand for a minimum wage was met with a compromise deal falling far short of what they had expected' (Dabb 1995, n.pag.). As a result, over 180,000 miners went out on strike in the biggest mining dispute since 1926.[3]

Simon Heffer of the *Daily Mail*, still angry 70 years after the end of the war, believed that

> for many trades unionists, the two world wars offered the perfect opportunity to blackmail their employers and the government into giving them better terms and conditions of service, and for expanding union power, with the threat that the country would suffer if the government and their employers didn't give in. (2015, n.pag.)

The war did offer the 'perfect opportunity' for workers and trade unionists to lobby for better 'terms and conditions of service', but to suggest that this was blackmail is simply untrue. Rather than seeing these strikes as 'the war's most shameful secret'—part of Heffer's title—they can be viewed as the working populace, as a result of labour conditions during the war, coming together to 'recognise a different kind of unity' (Dabb 1995, n.pag.). This unity helped contribute to the higher expectations of the British public and to the spate of sweeping reforms that the Labour government began to implement after their election win in 1945: the introduction of the NHS;

---

[3] Dabb goes on to make the barely believable claim that there had been such a decline in safety standards in the mining industry that by 1944 it 'meant that you had more chance of being injured as a miner than if you were fighting in the armed forces!' (1995, n.pag.).

the nationalisation of the coal, rail and dock industries; the repeal of the 1927 Trade Union act.

As previously mentioned, most strike histories in the UK jump from the 1926 General Strike to the 1972 miners' strike, following a route of equating the number of working days lost with a more general sense of social, cultural and economic importance. We attach such importance to the notion of lost working days due to strike action as it is by way of such measures that we consider the more explicit, demonstrable impact that trade unions can have. It also follows that the greater the number of working days lost, the greater the impact on the economy. However, by setting up our thinking in this way, we are in danger of coming to consider trade unions as simply a 'disruptive' force—the greater the disruption, the more importance given to the event. This 'quantitative' process is useful in so much as it allows us to measure what unions do or have done, but what this neglects is the types of legacies these disputes produce. This book explores the more 'qualitative' legacies of these disputes through poems that can be seen as questioning these received narratives and histories.

*

In terms of post-war mining and the larger industrial disputes of the late twentieth century, it was not until 1972 that another national coal strike was called. Here, miners were looking for a significant increase in their pay. While only 58.8 per cent of miners originally voted to go on strike—just exceeding the 55 per cent required—when it was called, 'not a single miner broke the strike. No one ever shouted "scab", for there was no one to shout it at' (Beckett & Hencke 2009, 23). It took the miners only a month to bring Britain to a halt: on 9 February Prime Minister Edward Heath was forced to declare a 'state of emergency', with the three-day working week following two days later. The strike was finally called off two weeks after (on 25 February) with the miners agreeing to a wage increase of between £5 to £6, plus other benefits ('1972: Miners Call Off Crippling Coal Strike' 2015).

This agreement was only a temporary fix in mining/government relations. On 1 February 1974—with Arthur Scargill now on the National Union of Mineworkers' (NUM) National Executive Committee, President of the Yorkshire Miners and pushing for industrial action—81 per cent of miners voted for strike action and Britain's miners were on strike again. This time things moved more swiftly. With the strike starting on 9 February, Heath called a snap election for the 25th of the month on the issue of 'who ran the country'. With Heath's subsequent defeat by Labour in the 1974 elections, the miners' union had effectively toppled the incumbent government and, through the work of the new Harold Wilson Labour government, the strike was brought to a timely end.

After the Second World War, trade union numbers continued to grow. Yet the attitudes from the trade union movement towards women and workers from minority backgrounds remained regressive. Nicole Busby and Rebecca Zahn, in their essay 'Women's Labour and Trade Unionism', quote from the Trades Union Congress's (TUC) annual report from 1948 which states:

> There is little doubt in the minds of the General Council that the home is one of the most important spheres for a woman worker and that it would be doing a great injury to the life of the nation if women were persuaded or forced to neglect their domestic duties in order to enter industry particularly where there are young children to cater for. (2016, n.pag.)

While the number of women who were members of a trade union continued to increase, and since 2005 women have made up the majority of the trade union membership—approximately 3.66 million women to 2.78 million men in the most recent statistics (Department for Business, Energy and Industrial Strategy 2022)—the trade union movement has historically not shown a great consideration for the specific needs of women. While women 'are often in industries with a high rate of turnover', with such industries 'noted for difficulty in organizing and militancy', it was the 1968 Ford Sewing Machinists' Strike and their campaign for equal pay, later recounted in the film *Made in Dagenham*, that led to the passing of the Equal Pay Act 1970. However, even when, in 1975, a 'Working Women's Charter, listing aims such as day centres, abortion, and family allowances, was debated at the 1975 TUC Congress', it was voted down by 'a card vote of 6,224,000 to 3,697,000 because many felt its provisions were outside the functions of the Congress' (Soldon 1985, 27). These issues are something that the poems themselves fail to address. There is a strain of masculinity that runs through the trade union movement that also informs the poems in this work. The narrative of unions is still a masculine one.

Similarly, the struggles experienced by minoritized workers are often sidelined in trade union narratives. The increase in the number of immigrants to the UK's workforce in the post-war years, particularly from the Commonwealth and those countries that had only recently extricated themselves from colonial rule, was beginning to change the face of employment in the UK. This change was not something the union movement was quick to recognise, or welcome. Ron Ramdin's groundbreaking 1987 book *The Making of the Black Working Class in Britain* talks of the Courtaulds Red Scar Mill in Preston where a strike was called 'over management's decision to force Asian workers to man more machines for proportionately less pay' (2017, 269).[4] The strike was to end in defeat. The Transport and General Workers' Union (TGWU) Chairman at the factory, Richard Roberts, called the strike 'unofficial' and 'racial'. As a result, the immigrant workers, although supported by the Indian Workers Association amongst others, 'failed to win against their oppressive employers, because of lack of union support' (Ramdin 2017, 271). In the instance of the 1974 Imperial typewriters' strike, the focus on recruiting Asian workers after 1968 had contributed to a turnover in 1972 more than treble that of 1968. Yet by 1974 bonuses were being renegotiated downwards, and 'to further reduce labour costs, more women were employed', as 'Asian women workers were regarded by the multinational employers as passive' (Ramdin 2017, 273). When the workers reached out to their union—the TGWU, and its negotiator George Bromley—they were harshly rebuked. Bromley wrote to the strikers saying: 'You are ill-led and have done nothing but harm to the company, the union and yourselves' (Dhondy quoted in Ramdin 2017, 273). The TGWU never made the strike legal. Most of the strikers were sacked and the trade union movement stayed largely silent on the whole matter.

The most momentous of the strikes involving minoritized workers was the 1976–8 Grunwick dispute. On 20 August 1976, a group of workers from the mail order department, made up predominantly of South Asian women and students from East Africa, walked out of the Grunwick Film Processing Laboratories in Willesden, London. In the mail order section, workers could expect compulsory overtime, unrealistic targets and, through the summer months, stifling heat. The strike lasted almost two years and would prove to be one of the most militant in British history, resulting in 550 arrests, more than any dispute since the 1926 General Strike (Ramdin 2017, 280). The workers, without union recognition at the time, turned to APEX (the Association of Professional, Executive, Clerical and Computer Staff). On 24 August, 'the initial sixty or so Grunwick workers completed their membership forms and were officially enrolled' in the union; by 31 August 'the number of strikers was 137 [...] out of a total workforce of about 490' (Rogaly 1977, 17, 19). The unions, finally, backed the workers. With the strike approaching the one-year mark the Grunwick

---

[4] The title is a response to E.P. Thompson's *The Making of the English Working Class* which, Ramdin felt, 'had entirely overlooked the presence and contribution of Black leaders who were prominent in English working-class struggles' (2017, xii). In his preface, Ramdin makes clear how he is using the terms 'black' and 'working class' in the work: 'In general, "black" refers to non-white persons, particularly those from former colonial and Commonwealth countries [...] "Working class" refers essentially to those unskilled and semi-skilled Blacks who came to Britain through the period, but particularly during the heavy post-war immigration in search of jobs' (2017, x).

Strike Committee called for a 'day of action', and 20,000 people and trade unionists, including the Yorkshire miners led by Arthur Scargill, marched through the town.

Yet, as time passed and victory began to look less likely, the support from APEX and UPW (Union of Post Office Workers) began to falter (Ramdin 2017, 302–3). As with so many of the labour disputes mentioned here, the Grunwick strike ended without victory for the workers. There were to be a few final, and occasionally violent, pushes before the dispute's end. On 7 November, 8,000 people turned out to protest and, after clashes with police, '243 pickets were treated for injuries, 12 had broken bones and 113 were arrested' (Bell and Mahmood 2016, n.pag.). With union support all but removed at this point, on 21 November, Jayaben Desai, the strike's 'leader', and three others went on hunger strike outside of the TUC offices in London. A call to renew the mass picketing in April 1978 failed, and the strike officially ended on 14 July 1978 in defeat and with something of a whimper.

*

In the lead up to the 1979 general election, Prime Minister James Callaghan, who had succeeded Harold Wilson in 1976, proved unable to appease the public-sector unions over their requests for increased wages, leading to what the newspapers called the 'Winter of Discontent'. The 'huge public sector strikes of the winter of 1978–9' which followed were 'fatal' to Callaghan's electoral prospects. The result was a win for a Thatcher-headed Conservative government 'far more radical' than Britain had ever known (Beckett & Hencke 2009, 26). A Conservative government who, according to Seumas Milne, once Director of Strategy for the Labour Party, were

> determined to break the back of the entire trade-union movement. The NUM was not the only powerful union in the establishment's sights—the giant Transport and General Workers' Union, with its hold on the docks and road transport, for example was also singled out for special treatment during the Thatcher years. But the NUM's unique industrial position, its unmatched radicalization, and the Conservative Party's spectacular humbling at the miners' hands left little question as to which union would become the new government's most important target. (2014, 7)

Through the 1980s, the Thatcher government was successful in radically reducing the membership numbers of trade union organisations, from 12.6 million in 1980 to 9.8 million by 1990; the NUM and the miners faced a government that would actively attempt to eradicate both them and their industry over the course of the next decade.

Over the next few years, Thatcher's government spent billions of pounds on improving Britain's nuclear power capacities, as well as increasing coal imports with the aim of unseating 'King Coal', in a Britain where roughly 80 per cent of 'electricity was generated from domestic coal'. The government built up stocks of domestic coal, introduced 'dual coal-oil firing at all power stations', withdrew 'social security benefits from strikers' families' and created a 'large, mobile squad of police' (Milne 2014, 9). By the time a strike was finally called by Arthur Scargill in March 1984—after the National Coal Board Chairman Ian MacGregor had informed 'the unions nationally of plans to cut four million tonnes of capacity and make 20,000 men redundant' (Beckett & Hencke 2009, 47)—the Tories were more prepared to fight the NUM than they had been in 1972 and 1974. It was estimated that to win, the miners 'would have had to stay on strike for a minimum of eighteen months' (McSmith 2011, 159). In the end they managed a year: a year that proved to be singular in its brutality. Documents released by the National Archives and published by the *Guardian* newspaper show that at a meeting with backbench Conservative MPs, Margaret Thatcher compared the 'battle' with the miners to Britain's war over the Falkland/Malvinas Islands in 1982, declaring:

> We had to fight the enemy without in the Falklands. We always have to be aware of the enemy within, which is much more difficult to fight and more dangerous to liberty. (Thatcher, qtd. in Travis 2013, n.pag.)

Margaret Thatcher's callous equation of the striking miners with the Argentine junta shows both the enormity of the threat she believed the miners posed to her (and her government) and the lengths to which she would go to quash any strike; by the end of the strike on 3 March 1985 the NUM 'put the overall death total at 11, along with 7,000 injured, 11,000 miners arrested and 1,000 miners sacked for their part in the strike' (McSmith 2011, 162). Not only did Thatcher crush the strike, she also crushed the mining industry in Britain:

> [I]n 1983 there were around 174 operational deep-mine pits in the UK, employing a total workforce of over 230,000 people. At the time of writing, Spring 2013 [...] there are now just three [...] employing barely 2000 miners. (Paterson 2014, 11)

Today there are no deep-pit mines left in the UK. Deep-pit mining in the UK came to an end on 18 December 2015, when the Kellingley pit in North Yorkshire closed. Paterson's words have an air of nostalgia that is not so present in the poems, at least in regard to the work of the miners. In 'Arthur Scargill', Ely writes of miners and their 'crushed torsos' and 'blood-streaked phlegm' (2013, 71). There is no nostalgia for the punishing work of mining, but there is for the perceived security and sense of community that it provided—'health and Palma de Mallorca / Cortinas on the drive and kids in college' (Ely 2013, 71). These were jobs that were supposed to last forever.

The strike of 1984–5 differed from those of the previous decade as they were not driven by disputes regarding pay and conditions, 'but about pit closures, unemployment and the survival of mining communities under widely varying degrees of threat' (Milne 2014, 17). These were communities which relied on and were inextricably linked to an industry that was in the process of being dismantled.

'Official' trade union histories in the UK are, again, quiet on the period after the end of the miners' strike of 1984–5.[5] Perhaps this is to be expected, since trade union membership figures dropped almost continually from the end of the strike in 1985 to the present day. One of the most notable strikes of the period was the Wapping print workers dispute in 1986–7 in which roughly 5,500 workers from Rupert Murdoch's newspaper printing plants went on strike. Murdoch, owner of the News International company which included *The Times*, *Sun* and other newspapers, had shifted newspaper production to a new, modern printing facility in Wapping. Along with the move, Murdoch said 'the company would be reducing the workforce in half a year from 5,500 to 1,500' (Littleton 1992, 76). Murdoch was successful. After the defeat of the miners only a few years earlier, this proved another blow to the trade union movement. Murdoch enjoyed almost complete support from the Thatcher government. The dispute exposed the unions' relative lack of power and the collusion between the media and the government. Perhaps of even greater consequence was the damage to the public perception of the power the unions held.

Since 2000, much of the larger-scale strike action has been called as a result of below-inflation wage increases or pension reforms in the public sector that would leave workers worse off at retirement. Yet the public and media perception of these strikes has rarely been positive, with unions having come to be viewed as, at best, unnecessarily disruptive or, at worst, an irrelevance. The end of 2002 saw the first firefighters' dispute since the 1970s, a dispute that arose after local authorities offered a 4 per cent pay rise in response to the Fire Brigades Union's call for a 39 per cent increase in wages. With the military stepping in to provide essential services, the strike finally petered out in June 2003—'the public, firefighters, employers and government seemed fed up with the dispute and the agenda had

---

[5] As in footnote 2 of this chapter, for the period 1984 to the present, the Office for National Statistics only includes the 2011 public-sector strikes in its history of industrial action in the UK ('The History of Strikes in the UK' 2015).

How Did We Get Here? The History

started to move on to bigger stories—Iraq and the toppling of Saddam Hussein' (Wright 2012, n.pag.). The firefighters finally agreed to a 16 per cent pay increase over three years. In 2007, the main postal union, the Communication Workers Union, walked out its 130,000 members over job security fears and modernisation plans. Four years later there were public-sector strikes over changes to pensions. Unions estimated that two million public sector workers went on strike—even though the Prime Minister, David Cameron, disputed these numbers and called the strike 'a damp squib' ('Strike Is a Damp Squib—Cameron' 2011). During the strike, 62 per cent of England's state schools were shut, while in Scotland only 33 of the 2,700 state schools remained open, and thousands of NHS operations were cancelled or postponed ('Public Sector Strike Rallies Held across UK' 2011). A YouGov poll carried out in June 2011, a few months before the strikes, found that only 40 per cent of respondents supported teachers going on strike over pensions, while a similar 38 per cent supported civil servants striking (Moran & Thompson 2011). On a smaller scale, the 2015 tube drivers' strike brought parts of London to a halt over plans to introduce a night underground service, with pictures of thousands of commuters queuing for buses giving the strike a unique visual presence. This strike action from a number of the country's foremost public services demonstrates a labour force whose livelihoods are under threat. It shows a union movement still integral to defending the basic rights and conditions of workers, but a union movement that is no longer connecting with large swathes of the population. For many, strikes are not viewed as the last resort of a desperate workforce, but as an inconvenience to those who no longer see the benefit of collective action and union organisations.

This brings us to the present and the 2016 Trade Union Act. While the number of days lost through strike action and trade union membership numbers continue to decrease, the passing of the Trade Union Act 2016 demonstrated that for those in government, and specifically the Conservative Party, unions were still seen as organisations whose potential to mobilise a populace was to be feared, and was in need of curbing. The government's press release upon the passing of the Act said that, with its introduction, 'people will be protected from undemocratic industrial action' and that these 'modernising reforms' would 'ensure strikes can only go ahead as a result of a clear and positive democratic mandate from union members: upholding the ability to strike while reducing disruption to millions of people' ('Trade Union Act Becomes Law' 2016). Although the government framed the Trade Union Act in terms of protecting 'millions of people', in actuality this is a significant restriction of workers' protections and their ability to use one of the final bargaining chips that they possess: the right to strike. The Act introduced a 50 per cent turnout threshold requirement so that at least half of those entitled to vote must do so for any union action to be lawful.⁶ In 'important public services', the restrictions were even more binding in that 40 per cent of all those who were entitled to vote must vote 'yes' to industrial action.⁷ In the 2016 referendum on leaving the European Union, only 37.4 per cent of eligible voters cast their ballot for 'leave'. Had the same thresholds been applied to the EU referendum vote as the government's trade union legislation for workers in 'important public services', the vote to leave the European Union would have been void. So, why is it that we hold our trade unions to a standard that we simply do not in other areas of governance?⁸

The answer lies in a sense of collective power. In a UK in which neoliberal ideas, and the competitive individualism that they bring, are still the driving force of our politics, the idea of a trade union is a powerful one. In an article in the *Telegraph* from 2017, Kate McCann claims that Labour 'would take the UK back to the 1970s' if elected, as it had revealed that it would 'enforce the right to trade union membership in every workplace across the country' and would call 'for a return to collective bargaining', perhaps even going so far as to extend the policy so that 'pay deals are set on an industry-wide basis' (McCann 2017, n.pag.). Labour did not win the 2017 general election, nor the 2019 one, yet what is interesting about McCann's article is that the phrase 'strike' is only mentioned once. It is the right to union membership and collective bargaining that is the focus of the piece. It is the fear of a workforce organising as a collective which is at the heart of the article. The Trade Union Act is itself as much about undermining the bonds that unions have with their members (or potential members) as it is about strike action—it strikes at the working class as a community. These union narratives are important because they play into the way we think of ourselves as workers, of the rights that we have, of the conditions we are willing to tolerate and the power we have to change and fight for these things. Readdressing and re-examining these narratives is a

---

⁶ By law, trade unions must conduct ballots by post, and are the only institutions that must do so in the UK.
⁷ The 'important public services' outlined by the Act are: '(a) health services; (b) education of those aged under 17; (c) fire services; (d) transport services; (e) decommissioning of nuclear installations and management of radioactive waste and spent fuel; (f) border security' (*Trade Union Act 2016, c.15, 2*).
⁸ Even if ballots to strike were successful, unions must now give two weeks' notice in advance of industrial action, as opposed to the one week that was previously necessary. Again, while not immediately contentious, this provision means that workplaces have additional time to prepare for any potential disruption a strike may cause and to implement measures to minimise any actual 'interruption' the strike itself might have. Therefore, when coming to the negotiating table, unions are invariably in a worse position.

step towards reconfiguring our position as workers, as workers who can be active participants in their labour representation.

The kinds of work we do affect how we think about ourselves in the world, the positions we hold within a society. In many instances, work connects us to or disconnects us from the places and spaces we inhabit. The question 'what do you do?' is second only to 'what's your name?' when people meet for the first time. Trade unions are not perfect, nor close to being perfect. However, many of the working provisions and protections that are taken for granted are the result of the efforts and struggles of the trade union movement. This chapter has recounted some of the major union events and disputes of the past century. It is shaped by facts and statistics as one way of telling and understanding our recent union histories. The rest of this book focuses on poetry.

The poets in this study are responding to a sense that the established narrative within which strikes are both justifiable and effective is coming under threat—first, by the mobilisation of anti-union narratives and popular hostility and, secondly (later on), by the de-unionisation of the workforce and the casualisation of the labour market. The poems regarding trade unionism can present to us alternative voices, question and probe prevailing narratives, and allow us to consider trade unions through a cultural form that is itself often outside mainstream and 'official' narratives. These poems highlight the ways in which our histories are performed and constructed, and the way in which dominant narratives seek (and have come) to control the representations of our industrial legacies. These poems allow for a more human, less economically and statistically minded interpretation of events. They perform the fractures in these narratives. They exploit the spaces which dominant narratives seek to obscure. Poetry says that language is contested, that it is part of the dispute itself. Poetry is an interrogation of language. This interrogation encourages us to consider subjects anew, to consider more than linear histories. By questioning the way we write about these narratives, we can question the narratives themselves.

CHAPTER TWO

Unions and Not Unions

> I restate my desire to follow in the footsteps of my father, the station restates its desire to refuse, I threaten to call in the union, the station says that's my prerogative. I remember that I'm not a member of a union and I hate unions.
>
> Alan Partridge, *Nomad* (2016)

I. Unions

It may be obvious, but a worker does not have to be a member of a trade union, and today that is true for the majority of those in employment. A union is an organisation which workers join voluntarily, on the condition of paying a membership fee, to be eligible for the benefits which unionisation affords—centred around working conditions, job security and pay. A trade union's primary aim is to protect the interests of its members, or workers more generally. Yet the varied interaction of members with their union, and the range of reasons workers have for joining a union, means that any homogeneous representation of trade union members and membership is only ever an oversimplification.

Owen Jones writes in *Chavs: The Demonization of the Working Class* that 'the unions, whatever their faults and limitations, had given the workers in [old industrial] communities strength, solidarity and a sense of power. All of this had sustained a feeling of belonging, of pride in a shared working-class experience' (2012, 48–9). These members are 'workers' in 'communities' as much as part of a union movement. Yet, for Jones, unions' ability to supply workers with the 'sense of power' and security afforded by being part of a union is passing. It is this distinction between workers as members of a trade union and workers as individuals that this chapter will explore, in regard to the formation of strike narratives.

Unions and Not Unions

*

This chapter will focus on what can broadly be seen as three poetic 'moments' in regard to trade unions' presence in UK poetry; the first, with the work of Barry MacSweeney, covering the era following the 1974 miners' strike; the second examining poetry produced in response to the 1984–5 miners' strike, specifically the work of Tony Harrison and Sean O'Brien; and the third, which does not come directly out of any major industrial dispute, covering 2010 to 2015, with particular reference to collections by Steve Ely and Helen Mort.

1.1 Barry MacSweeney's Black Torch and 'Black Torch Sunrise'
MacSweeney's 1978 collection *Black Torch* is composed of a number of 'sections'. Andrew Duncan reads these sections as

> a dedication to Eric Mottram; an account of (probably two) miners' strikes in 1854 occupying the bulk of the book; a poem about a girl, Pearl, set in the 1950s, a legend, 'Melrose to South Shields', slipped in; 'Black Lamp Strike', a poem about many different seditious and protest activities in around 1817; and a final poem, 'Black Torch Sunrise', set in the present day of 1977, with the poet watching television and talking about politics. (2013, 64)

It is clear that labour and politics are at the heart of this collection—'nee schools or churches / so miners set up their own' (MacSweeney 1978, 21). If, as Andrew Duncan claims, 'most textbooks were really histories of the political elite in the south-east', *Black Torch* with its focus on Northumberland and Durham can be seen as alleviating or, at the least, starting from, this position of historical 'silence' (2013, 72). In MacSweeney's collection, the history of the north-east is intrinsically bound up with labour and trade unions.

Black Torch's final poem, 'Black Torch Sunrise', concerns itself with the way in which news is reported. MacSweeney said that the poem came about after 'listening for twenty-four hours, non-stop, to the BBC World Service' (2019, n.pag.). The poem opens with a television showing reports of a 'riot' in Paris:

> BBC monochrome newsreel flickers
>   jerking on small family TV screen—
> Sorbonne students hoy parking meters
>   paving stones ripped, military phalanx
> lowers grinning plexiglass
> bodies' confrontation on sensual Paris boulevards
> tolerated hash on Amsterdam cuts down riot-quota.

The poem opens with the BBC—prior to which we have a dedication to the poet Tom Pickard and an epigraph from Allen Ginsberg's 'Eclogue'. The BBC and the 'monochrome newsreel' establishes the tone of the poem.[1] In the next stanza, the first pronoun is introduced, coming from the BBC's reportage of what 'our correspondent says':

> our correspondent says there will be no
>   repetition of the 1968 near-revolution
>   because students have not gained support
>   of the French working-class. (MacSweeney 1978, 71)

This section is a newsreader relaying information from the correspondent to the public. There is a sense of 'ownership' over the correspondent and that the BBC owns this interpretation of the news. The BBC controls the news narrative. We are presented with a filtering of information from the correspondent to BBC, and then BBC to the audience watching the news. The authority exists with the BBC. By choosing to report what the correspondent has said, but leaving the correspondent as an unnamed source, space is created in which the BBC can distance itself from the report. If the narrative were to shift or be reconfigured, the 'responsibility' for the report becomes someone else's. Yet the circumstances that led to the 1968 'near-revolution' are still present and the responses to it are still the same. The BBC is using the images and narratives of the past to justify (and pre-empt) the actions of the political present (and future).

It is the BBC that decides who has the authority to be heard. In a letter to the *New Statesman* in 1979, Richard Francis, then Director of News and Current Affairs at the BBC, wrote that the BBC's journalists 'find it natural to ask "an important person"—a senior civil servant or government minister, for instance—for they are the people whose decisions largely determine how things will be run in our democracy'. The letter posits a class assumption, continued by journalists, 'that some people are more important than others and have a greater right to speak' (Philo 1982, 138). As a result of such assumptions, the BBC is complicit in maintaining the social status quo.[2] In MacSweeney's poem,

---

[1] As mentioned earlier, 'Black Torch Sunrise' was written after MacSweeney had been listening to the BBC World Service, which he described as being 'very good' but 'slightly bizarre' because it was, as he saw it, a 'propaganda service' (2019, n.pag.).

[2] At the outset of the 1975 British Leyland Motor Corporation's engine tuners' (unofficial) strike in Cowley, Oxfordshire, the Prime Minister, Harold Wilson, gave a speech referring to 'manifestly avoidable stoppages of production'. Across the three television channels (BBC1, BBC2 and ITN) strikes came to be presented as the 'main problem facing the car industry in general and British Leyland Motor

Unions and Not Unions

it is through the BBC's reporting that the claim is made that there 'will be no / repetition of the 1968 near-revolution' (MacSweeney 1978, 71); this becomes the 'state-sponsored' viewpoint, it is the line that is to be repeated, it is the story that is broadcast.

The next section introduces both the Labour Party and the Trades Union Congress (TUC):

> Leftists mount insurrection
>   neat covert agents ensure safety
>   When does 'made payments'
>   become 'offered bribes'?
> Will the Labour Party uphold the jailing of pickets?
> Of course.
>
> —TUC inner cadres make closed door pacts with the Govt
> This allows the £
>   some relief on the European market
>   Bank of England dwarfs
> up the lending rate
>   affording confidence
>   to other dwarfs. (MacSweeney 1978, 71)

Taking the assertion that there 'will be no / repetition' in conjunction with the line 'TUC inner cadres make closed door pacts with the Govt', it becomes more difficult to ascertain who is making these claims. We are never told from whom or how the 'correspondent' gleaned their information. The line about the TUC becomes one in which MacSweeney is interrogating the role of the TUC as an institution and questioning the claims put forward by a media set on condemning union action.

'Black Torch Sunrise' is the only poem in the volume in which a union organisation is referenced by name. The TUC is not technically a trade union, but a federation which represents the majority of trade union organisations in the UK. Its mission is to 'be a high profile organisation that campaigns successfully for trade union aims and values; assists trade unions

---

Corporation in particular' (Beharrell 1976, 256–7). This view of the dispute came to dominate the news agenda with '42 references (to the strike and Wilson's speech) emphasising this interpretation'; compared with the 'dominant' view of the strike, Jack Jones criticising Leyland's management 'received three references on BBC1, none on BBC2 and three on ITN' (Beharrell 1976, 263). Even though these numbers are massively weighted in favour of the government's view of events, these figures may still, according to Peter Beharrell, overstate 'the actual emphasis given to alternative explanations', as 'information which contradicts the dominant view tends to be discounted, sandwiched or overwhelmed' (1976, 266).

to increase membership and effectiveness; cuts out wasteful rivalry; and promotes trade union solidarity' ('About the TUC' 2015). Yet, following the question 'Will the Labour Party uphold the jailing of pickets?', the TUC becomes an explanation for the answer, 'of course'. It is the TUC making 'pacts' with the government that allows this 'jailing of pickets'. In the poem, MacSweeney contrasts the plight of individual trade unionists with the behaviour of the 'inner cadre' of the collective TUC. The members are the ones who suffer. The 'closed door pacts' suggest that the TUC is aware of the Labour Party's intentions to jail striking workers.[3]

The 'TUC', through the capitalised acronym, is visually linked with the 'BBC', a public-service organisation that is connected to the state through its funding from the television licence fee. Similarly, the TUC is bound to the government through its 'pact' and certain legislations as to how it can and cannot operate. The TUC acts as an intermediary between the government and the trade unions it represents, but the 'pact' is made with the government, the unions themselves are absent. MacSweeney's 'cadre' suggests an activist front to the TUC, but that, in actuality, there is an 'inner' cohort within the TUC who control the dynamic between the unions and the government. The public narrative may be one of activism (and strikes), but the private is one of collusion and compromise.

The following section begins with the lines:

> Circles broken circumferences ripped
>   perimeters buckled
> facts revealed
>   must be published
> because they are seditious. (MacSweeney 1978, 71)

---

[3] The phrase 'closed door pacts' is a reference to the Liaison Committee, established in 1972, which brought together the TUC and the Labour Party to work out a 'common programme for action if Labour won the next general election' (Taylor 2000, 209). After Labour's win in 1974, the Social Contract grew out of the Labour Party's acceptance of trade union power after the 1972 and 1974 miners' strikes, in the context of the need to stabilise the British economy. The Social Contract, a policy that ran roughly from 1974 to 1978, 'committed the government to policies the unions wanted—the repeal of the Industrial Relations Act, increased spending on welfare benefits, state-imposed restrictions on the prices of essentials—in return for an undertaking from the unions to accept modest pay rises, agreed with the government, which would not worsen the inflation rate and the already perilous economic situation' (Beckett 2009, 291). Although these aims may seem to show a government actively committed to improving the lot of the working class, 'wage increases for union members had been consistently at or below the rate of inflation […] The result was a brutal cut in the standard of living of some of the Labour Party's most natural and loyal supporters' (Beckett 2009, 436).

The 'closed' pacts from the previous lines have been 'ripped' open from the outside. With 'buckled', we are presented with a tension between closing and opening under pressure. Yet the circle of the pact is broken and the 'facts' of the meeting are exposed. These 'facts', the speaker tells us, 'must be published / because they are seditious' (MacSweeney 1978, 71). The facts to be 'revealed' are 'seditious', but so are the organisations of the TUC and government themselves. The facts 'need to be published' because they expose the complicity between the TUC and the government. While these facts have been forced into the open, they have 'buckled'. There is a warping of the facts and, simultaneously, a closing in, in an attempt to secure them. Here, the media coexists with the TUC and the government. These 'facts' and the issues surrounding them arise out of the cooperation between all three organisations. The exhortation 'must' does not imply that the facts are to be published, but that the need for them to be is essential. The 'facts' have been revealed, but the poem does not give us to whom. These 'facts' exist within the poem, but there is the suggestion that they will not make it to the news cycle or as far as the wider public. MacSweeney shows the TUC as being both complicit with the media and government in the establishment of these 'official narratives', while also being at the mercy of this dissemination (or failed dissemination) of 'official narratives' and political messages.

I.II Tony Harrison's 'V.'

The second poetic moment, approximately 1984–9, arises out of the struggle and subsequent failure of the UK miners' strike of 1984–5. Of all the poetry which could be seen as having a trade union interest, none has been more widely discussed or caused more controversy than Tony Harrison's 'V.' (1985). The 'v.' represents the notions of victory, versus and verses negotiated throughout the 3,500-word poem. It opens up a number of meanings, between 'versus' as a battle still in progress and 'victory' as some form of satisfactory conclusion to said battle. These are also the 'verses' of poetry. This ambiguity establishes the poem as one of contestation, where what it means to produce poetry and construct narratives is challenged. Through the poem's title, Harrison is questioning exactly who and what it is that controls our language choices and narratives, and the extent to which language can be appropriated and moulded to be used both as an inclusive and exclusive tool.

Harrison wrote 'V.' 'in a vandalised cemetery in Leeds during the Miners' Strike' (Harrison 2008, 35). He begins the poem with a quotation from a man who was, at the time, probably Britain's most recognisable Yorkshireman and striker, Arthur Scargill: 'My father still reads the dictionary every day. He says your life depends on your power to master words' (Harrison 2008, n.pag.). Scargill quoting his father ties in with the poem's concerns regarding language and parentage, with Harrison going to visit his family's graveyard plot and finding 'UNITED graffitied' on his parents' gravestone (2008, 12). 'United' suggests a common purpose, yet here it exposes a form of separation. There is a physical separation between the writer or narrator (Harrison) and the deceased (his parents), the linguistic ambiguity of the graffiti and the concept of union itself.

In the poem, there is a division between the language we expect, particularly of poetry, and the language and narratives we are presented with. What is interesting in regard to trade unions is that the Scargill epigraph to the poem is included without any biographical explanation as to who Scargill is: what we see is the 'removal' of the union organisation from the individual. There is only one section in which there is a direct reference to a trade union, and it is, unsurprisingly, the NUM:

> Vs sprayed on the run at such a lick,
> the sprayer master of his flourished tool,
> get short-armed on the left like that red tick
> they never marked his work much with at school.
>
> Half this skinhead's age but with approval
> I helped whitewash a V on a brick wall.
> No one clamoured in the press for its removal
> or thought the sign, in wartime, rude at all.
>
> These Vs are all the versuses of life
> from LEEDS v. DERBY, Black/White
> and (as I've known to my cost) man v. wife,
> Communist v. Fascist, Left v. Right,
>
> class v. class as bitter as before,
> the unending violence of US and THEM,
> personified in 1984
> by Coal Board Macgregor and the NUM,
>
> Hindu/Sikh, soul/body, heart v. mind,
> East/West, male/female, and the ground
> these fixtures are fought out on's Man, resigned
> to hope from his future what his past never found. (Harrison 2008, 11)

The passage shows Harrison bombarding us with choices, conflicts and disputes, all managed through his use of three conjunctions: truncated 'v.', the forward slash ('/') and 'and'. Wojciech Klepuszewski, in his essay on the poem, claims that the 'small "v" becomes the common denominator in the poem [...] and carries a great polysemic weight: behind each of these v's lie problems pivoting around various political, cultural and social issues' (2011, 25). Klepuszewski's assertion has merit, especially with the idea of 'pivoting' in regard to the 'v.', but it ignores the aforementioned conjunctions. The letter 'v' is itself both united and divided, its arms extending out from a single unified point. We read 'LEEDS v. DERBY' in the same way as we read 'UNITED' graffitied on the gravestone. The internal 'v.' modulates our relationship to the two sides, putting them into conflict with one another and encouraging us to see this 'conflict' as existing only within this very narrow duality. 'LEEDS v. DERBY' could as easily be read in terms of the 1984–5 miners' strike—when over 97 per cent of Yorkshire miners went on strike, whereas in North Derbyshire only 66.7 per cent went out and in South Derbyshire it was 11 per cent (Richards 1996, 109). These sides are *put* into conflict with one another, the narrative being told is that they are in dispute. What Harrison is speaking to is the idea of positionality. We project or seek out a position (or one is forced upon us) that modulates our relationships with groups that are other to what we consider to be our own. We are told who we should be 'against'. This position then becomes one of the elements by which histories of a group come to be constructed.

In positioning the 'v' alongside 'and' and '/', Harrison is not only shifting the nature of each 'conflict', but also leading the reader to consider how we come to be socially positioned. The slash, as it is most commonly understood, functions in the same way as 'or' and projects an idea that the two (or more) categories arranged around them act as mutually exclusive. It is also a barrier, a line that one cannot cross. It is as if the slash is necessary to keep two things separate or to maintain difference that one might fear is being eroded. The categories that Harrison separates with a '/' initially appear to be those that you are born as or into. In the poem, there is an implication that we are forced to identify ourselves or others as one of the two options provided. We are only ever given the choice of two, meaning that we are engineered into a position where the impression of choice is still divided by a carefully delineated boundary, and further, a boundary that has only taken into 'consideration' labels imposed from the outside. This is the danger that Harrison appears to be exposing.

Where Harrison writes 'Hindu/Sikh', these two sides are presented as mutually exclusive. Indeed, in 1985, issues in India had effectively produced a binary of Hindu/Sikh or a 'Hindu v. Sikh' position. The 'Hindu/Sikh' reference relates to the 1984 Operation Blue Star, in which Indian Prime Minister Indira Gandhi ordered the storming of the Golden Temple, occupied by Sikh separatists. This led to her assassination by her own Sikh bodyguards at the end of October 1984—Gandhi was Hindu—and the 'anti-Sikh riots' later in 1984, where 'the Indian government suspended constitutional rights in Punjab and committed gross human rights abuses against tens of thousands of people' (Hundal 2009). What is omitted by Harrison is that many people are not, or do not subscribe to, any of the (other) binaries he presents the reader. Yet, by reading the forward slash as another form of conflict we bring the two 'binaries' into conversation with one another. By being in one of these categories you situate yourself within a larger community, but this categorisation can also separate you from other forms of identification; by being in conflict with something you become an active participant in the way the other group defines itself. The narrative of one group becomes inextricably bound with its 'rival' or 'counterpoint'. Harrison is suggesting that as these binaries are presented to us as absolute, we come to think of them as such, establishing our narratives around imposed labels and staged conflicts.

Turning to the strike aspect of the poem, Harrison positions the NUM around the conjunctive 'and':

> class v. class as bitter as before,
> the unending violence of US and THEM,
> personified in 1984
> by Coal Board MacGregor and the NUM. (2008, 11)

In this stanza, the shift from the abstract 'class' to the concrete organisation of 'the NUM' points, again, to problems of positioning. Taking the reading of 'LEEDS v. DERBY' from earlier, the initial implication is to read the first 'class' as the one to which you are nominally aligned. Although the two 'classes' are presented identically, they are not. The lack of differentiation between 'class v. class' evokes ideas of a people at war with themselves and echoes journalist and ex-Labour MP Brian Walden's words that the miners' strike of 1984–5 was 'a civil war without guns' ('Miners' Strike 1984–85: "A Civil War without Guns"' 2004). There is an open-endedness to the conflict, it is allowed to bleed into the rest of the line and into the wider concerns of the poem. Class becomes the genesis and justification for 'the unending violence' and aggression, equally attributable to both 'sides'—the violence 'justified' by a working class whose jobs are under threat, and a ruling class who are having their economic interests negatively affected by the miners' strike. If the class violence is 'as bitter as before', there is a suggestion that everyone already 'knows' which side they are on, however unclear this appears from the outside. This 'unending violence' is then read as a re-emergence of violence which has occurred in some abstract 'before'. This is a story that has been told before, the terms requiring no explanation. Yet these 'classes' across the 'v' justify one another. The 'v' only exists if there are two sides to the conflict. Each side creates the terms by which the other exists, while requiring the recognition of the other for its own existence.

Harrison's shift from 'class v. class' to 'US and THEM' and finally to 'Coal Board MacGregor and the NUM' is suggestive of questions around the institutional control of information and the ways in which different institutions or systems are represented. On the page, Harrison's two 'classes' are visually the same, yet readers will naturally align themselves with the one they *think* relates to them. The reader is left with the onus of positioning themselves within the class struggle. The difference between 'US and THEM' is easier to account for. 'US' removes the burden of having to account for what it actually includes or entails. There is an implicit belief that there is a shared experience of something that does need not to be elaborated on further. The 'us' is a fixed position which, while being made up of individuals, has a singular voice and singular social or political position. As a reader, the 'us' becomes whatever we want it to be, or, more precisely, whatever we perceive ourselves to be. We are co-opted by Harrison into positioning ourselves and deciding what it is our 'us' represents. Harrison demonstrates the ease by which our freedom to choose how we are perceived is essentially at the behest of other institutions and the language acts of others. Not only do we not exist outside of the language which we use to present ourselves, but the language that we use can be affixed to us without our consent. In the poem, all these constructions come out of the clash between the two appearances of the word 'class'. The two versions of the word are not the same, one has to come first. The 'class' with which you align is the arbitrary matter of the class you are born into.

As Harrison goes on to rhyme 'US and THEM' with 'Coal Board MacGregor and the NUM', any easy acceptance or comprehension of which side we reside on is exploded. Harrison is the most immediate instigator of the 'US'. It is he who is setting the initial limitations or qualifications which constitute it. Harrison has said that he 'was born into an uneducated working-class family in Leeds' and as a result of winning 'one of those scholarships created by the Education Act of 1944' to study at Leeds Grammar School, he was 'considered "bright" if nothing else' (2017, 169). The title for his second collection *From the School of Eloquence* (1978) is borrowed from E.P. Thompson's *The Making of the English Working Class* (1963). In the collection, Harrison's poem 'Them and [uz]' echoes 'US and THEM', with the order of the pronouns reversed. 'Them and [uz]' focuses its attention on the young Harrison attempting to broaden the vernacular by which poetry can be 'spoken', reinstating his Leeds-accented pronunciation of 'us' as /uz/ rather than the 'correct' Received Pronunciation version, /ʌs/ (Harrison 1995, 34). With this in mind, the 'US' from 'V.' becomes troubled, as Harrison is taking on a linguistic identifier he has already attempted to reject. 'US' cannot simply be viewed as Harrison co-opting the reader into his world view. Harrison's uneasiness with his own position becomes more pronounced. Indeed, it can be read as Harrison, the narrator, taking on an identity that Harrison, the poet, feels is being imposed on him. This imposition can be seen in Harrison's rhyming, against what we may believe his position or identity is in the poem, 'THEM' with 'NUM'.

Harrison is showing through his use of these dualities—'LEEDS v. DERBY, Black/White', etcetera—the way in which 'dominant' and 'alternative' politics and culture are inseparable from one another, regardless of the ways in which they may be oppositional or not. The poem can be seen as illuminating the inherent difficulties in determining what constitutes part of the hegemony and what can realistically be termed oppositional. Which parts of our narratives have come to be 'imposed' on us by dominant cultural processes and which parts try to question this established order? It is Harrison at all points who is creating this system of control, or perceived control and order, in the work. During 1984–5, the Scargill-headed NUM undoubtedly came to be seen as 'oppositional'. Harrison rhymes THEM/NUM in a way which troubles our sense of political affiliation. 'V.' is broadly a pro-strike poem. However, Harrison and most readers of the work are not (and would not have been) members of the NUM, regardless of how they view it. This mirroring of THEM/NUM shows Harrison to be speaking to the dangers of 'blind' associations, by uniformly relating two images or words because of their assumed aesthetic or linguistic relationship. What this association exposes is the way in which our histories come to be constructed for us, and the danger of us constructing our own narratives around these overly simplified groupings. Harrison's work is attempting to question a strike narrative that is already coming to be seen as 'absolute'. As a non-NUM member himself, to Harrison, the NUM and its members are 'THEM' and not 'US'.

Writing about 'Coal Board MacGregor and the NUM', Harrison frames the 1984–5 strike in terms of class struggle, whereby the 'Coal Board' stands for those who own and control the means of production and the 'NUM' represents the labour force behind production. Harrison personifies the Coal Board in the singular figure of Ian MacGregor, yet refers to the collective NUM—even more surprising considering the opening quotation of the poem comes from Arthur Scargill, who is not mentioned again in the work. Harrison is setting the singular drive of the industrialist MacGregor and the Coal Board against the collective struggle of unionised workers.[4] As Harrison uses the 'and' to connect the two sides involved in the strike— leaving out the political parties and figures who were prominent throughout the strike, Thatcher being the most glaring omission—he does so in such a fashion that the individual and the collective are viewed together. Although these two groups come to define 1984, at least in the UK and our prevailing history of the year, they are by no means the sum of it. MacGregor is presented as the personification of the Coal Board, in a show

---

[4] Ian MacGregor was head of the Coal Board during the 1984–5 strike. Having previously worked for British Steel and overseen the reduction of its workforce by over half at the end of the 1970s, it is clear what his objectives were when appointed.

of the reductionist nature of discussions surrounding the strike of 1984–5. MacGregor's own agency is removed by presenting him solely as a figure for the organisation he represents. MacGregor, while the representative of the Coal Board, does not account for the whole negative campaign against the miners; similarly, to pretend the NUM is simply a collective without any figures or hierarchy, is itself a misrepresentation. Having said this, although the NUM is a collective and garnered its power through its membership and representation of workers in an industry that was essential to the running of the UK, it has itself been reduced to an isolated group. Harrison has removed the strike from the realm of miners who are on strike to position it as being represented not by the people involved but by the institution that organised them. Harrison says that the NUM 'personified' class violence in 1984. Here there is an oversimplification about a group that is made up of individual, fee-paying members being treated simply as an abstract representation. The 'and' linking 'Coal Board MacGregor and the NUM' aligns the two bodies as similar corporate structures to be treated almost as equal in their aspirations. Harrison shows that societal groupings exist as cultural products as much as political ones. What is deemed either part of *our* social community or not depends on a narrative, which is necessarily unstable, of the power dynamics between the elements that constitute and challenge the view of who we are.

I.III Sean O'Brien's 'Summertime'
Although Sean O'Brien would later state that 'poetry does not court relevance, except to life's permanent conditions' (2006, 172), in his 1987 collection, *The Frighteners*, the 1984–5 miners' strike recurs throughout the book: 'Unregistered' concerns itself with the importation of 'coal to break the strike' from the Baltic during the dispute (23);[5] in 'London Road' the themes of state-organised violence and the 'rule of law' are addressed; while 'Cousin Coat' details the exploitation of the northern working poor. In 'Cousin Coat', O'Brien writes of there being 'no comfort when the strikers all go back / To see which twenty thousand get the sack' (1987, 47). The NUM may have called the strike, but it is the strikers who will lose their jobs. You go on strike as part of a union, but you lose your job as a 'striker', as an individual.

In this context, I want to briefly consider Sean O'Brien's 'Summertime', with its dedication 'for Richard Richardson, Kent NUM' (1987, 18). Even though *The Frighteners* includes a number of poems that are expressly about

---

[5] Surprisingly, considering they were communist states at the time, at Glasson dock, Lancashire, 'coal boats docked on every tide from East Germany and Poland, to be unloaded directly onto lorries queueing at the dock gates' (Winterton and Winterton 1989, 92).

the miners' strike of 1984–5, this is the only reference to a trade union in O'Brien's collection. This dedication is of note for a number of reasons, the first being that it is unusual to find a 1984–5 strike poem dedicated to a figure other than Arthur Scargill—'the trade union movement's one and only celebrity' (Milne 2014, 28)—and that at the end of the strike Jack Collins was the head of the Kent chapter of the NUM, not Richardson. O'Brien has said that:

> Richardson was from [the] Kent NUM, though I don't remember if I ever knew his precise role. He came and spoke to an NUT branch meeting when I was a teacher. He was an inspiring speaker, an older man, white-haired as I seem to recall. (personal communication, 27 Jan. 2016)

The choice of the Kent NUM is interesting, if only coincidental, as a result of the Kent NUM's stance at the strike's close. In March 1985, when the end of the strike appeared inevitable, it was the Kent chapter of the NUM that proposed to continue the strike, which 'was heavily defeated, 170 votes to 19' (Beckett 2009, 218). Jack Collins said of the event that 'the people who have decided to go back to work and leave men on the sidelines, to unload these men, are the traitors of the trade union movement' (qtd. in Beckett 2009, 219). O'Brien's decision to include the Kent NUM is politically charged: by specifying a branch of the NUM—a branch whose leader viewed much of the union as 'traitors' to the miners on strike and the 'trade union movement' as a whole—there is an implicit critique of the wider Union. What O'Brien does (that Harrison does not) is to reinstate the individual within the union narrative (even though Richardson is not mentioned again), and show that the NUM was at least geographically divided and should not be considered as a homogenous entity. The story of the strike is one that involves individuals, even if they have been sidelined. O'Brien contextualises his poem and his reading of the strike in terms of an individual, 'Richard Richardson', then via location ('Kent') and, finally, via a union ('NUM'). However, the poem opens with the phrase 'The news is old' and the figures of 'Richardson' or the trade union do not appear again:

> The news is old. A picket line
> Is charged and clubbed by mounted police.
> *Regrettable. Necessity.*
> *You have to take a balanced view.*
> *That kind of thing can't happen here*
> *And when it does it isn't true.* (O'Brien 1987, 18)

The story of the strike doesn't truly include Richardson. Although O'Brien dedicates the poem to 'Richardson', he is immediately sidelined by the 'official' strike narrative, one in which 'a picket line / is charged and clubbed by mounted police', as it is a *'Necessity'* (1987, 18). O'Brien's dedication to Richardson leaves him on the outskirts of the poem; he is part of it, but not an actor in the telling and retelling of the strike narrative. The narrative, as far as O'Brien sees it, is one that is already formed—'The news is old' (1987, 18)—and those involved in the strike are simply left to watch it be retold.

I.IV Steve Ely's 'Ballad of the Scabs', Irish Blood, English Heart' and 'Inglan is a Bitch'

The third 'poetic moment', running roughly from 2012 to 2015, firmly establishes itself in the territory of legacy. The strikes of the 1970s and 1980s are long finished and what we see are poems written in response to them, and dealing with their legacy.

Steve Ely's *Englaland* is described in its blurb as 'an unapologetic and paradoxical affirmation of a bloody, bloody-minded and bloody brilliant people. Danish huscarls, Falklands war heroes, pit-village bird-nesters, aging prize-fighters, flying pickets, jihadi suicide-bombers and singing yellowhammers'. In Ely's work, trade unions, strike action and violence underpin poems littered with acronyms from industry and politics. Much of Ely's union focus comes in the book's second movement, 'The Harrowing of the North'.[6]

'Ballad of the Scabs', the centrepiece and longest poem of 'The Harrowing of the North', works as a potted history of the NUM, and more broadly the miners' strikes, during the 1970s and '80s:

> In '72 the NUM
> shook the Tory State
> closing down the cokeworks
> there at Saltney Gate.
>
> The miners' flying pickets
> and their comrades in the TUC
> showed the power the workers have
> when they act in unity. (Ely 2015, 136)

The opening to the poem grants the NUM the power to destabilise the state. However, through the first two stanzas there is a gradual shift as we see 'the NUM' become 'miners' and then 'workers'. There is a tension

---

[6] 'The Harrowing of the North' refers to William I's—alternatively known as William the Conqueror or William the Bastard—Harrying of the North (1069–70), his brutal attempts to quell uprisings in the north of England. Ely draws a parallel between that event and the war against trade unions, and more specifically the NUM, during the miners' strikes of the 1970s and 1980s.

between the view of unions as homogenous organisations and unions as being composed of workers who often share the same profession but not necessarily the same views on how their unions should operate. The 1972 strike was predominantly about increasing wages for NUM members—albeit in an industry that had already seen hundreds of pit closures at the cost of approximately 430,000 jobs since the late 1950s ('NUM: Historic Speeches' 2015). Yet Ely chooses to focus on the broader political impact that the 1972 strike had on the 'Tory State'. This is an important distinction to make for it situates industrial action in direct opposition to the 'state' rather than, as seen in Harrison, the Coal Board. Ely's distinction elevates the 1972 miners' strike from an industrial dispute between employees and management to a conflict between workers and 'the state'. The union is situated as a political organisation, defined by its political, not labour-based, impact. Yet it is through stopping working and blockading their workplaces that unions have political efficacy. Unlike MacSweeney and Harrison, Ely presents the union as proactive, even if it is the NUM's ability to organise a withdrawal of labour, through picketing and strike action, that affords them the greatest political agency. In the poem's opening, the NUM are not defending their members' jobs or working conditions against the state; in fact the job of mining is not mentioned. The NUM are the aggressors whose main aim appears revolutionary.

In this verse, the NUM is 'replaced' as we shift from political concerns to more explicitly strike-based action. While it is unions that call industrial action, it is the members of the unions that must enact the strike, by withholding their labour and manning the picket lines. However, it is still the NUM which closes 'down the cokeworks', not the workers. Where the NUM 'shook' the state and is 'closing down' factories, the miners and 'their comrades' 'show' their power and 'act' in unity. As Ely terms this demonstration of unity an 'act', we have the twin ideas of performance and action being presented. This 'act' is one that is required for the presentation of unity that industrial action requires. The workers' actions, their labour, is still the most powerful thing they possess. Published in 2015, there is a sense that Ely is commenting not just on workers' unity in the early 1970s, but also on the decreasing influence of unions and the lack of collective organisation today. Ely is also serving a reminder of past union strength and arguing for a return to this position of collective organisation. By refashioning this NUM 'narrative', Ely's work is performing this 'noble' history of the NUM as a way of challenging present-day union narratives that seek to denounce industrial action as an irrelevance.

Ely continues his separation of union and worker in the verses that follow, with the union responsible for political change but workers forced to bear the weight of the repercussions that come from industrial action:

> In '74 they finished the job
> and forced out Edward Heath
> they chipped in from their pay rise
> to buy capital a wreath.
>
> The ruling class got nervous
> and planned a counter-attack
> to perpetate [*sic*] their power
> and put the workers on the rack. (2015, 136)

The 'they' at first appears to be a continuation of the 'workers' from the previous stanza. However, as the line echoes the opening of the poem, 'they' is amalgamated into both 'workers' and 'NUM'. As a result, the 'job' becomes somewhat ambiguous: the 'job' is that of forcing Edward Heath from power; there are two 'jobs', getting a 'pay rise' and forcing out Heath, both of which are equally important; or, there is the primary job—'pay rise'—and an unintended consequence, the end of Edward Heath's government. What these distinctions do is question what a union should be doing, what it should be for, and the interaction between 'regular' members and union officials. Ely attempts to provide an answer when he writes that 'they chipped in from their pay rise / to buy capital a wreath'. There is a certain sense of complacency (or even naivety) in the lines, since the pay rise is both a victory over and a result of 'capital', which is far from dead. In this reading, the workers and union become complicit with capital and the 'chipping in' becomes a way of giving thanks, rather than paying last respects. The workers are complicit in shaping a narrative that seeks to exclude them. There is a tension between being separated from and yet a part of a capitalist system that plagues trade union organisations. As Stanley Aronowitz states in his book on American labour unions: 'organized labor is integrated into the prevailing political and economic system; so much so that it not only complies with the law but also lacks an ideology opposed to the prevailing capitalist system' (2014, n.pag.). Aronowitz's judgement, of course, cannot be directly mapped onto British labour relations. Yet the 1972 and 1974 miners' strikes both complied with UK law and the aim of these strikes was not for workers to remove themselves from a capitalist system, but to be able to function more effectively within it through increased wages. It is ironic that, in Ely's poem, the first thing the workers do after receiving their pay rise is feed money back into the state.

In the poem, the state returns to attack the unions during the 1984–5 miners' strike, when attempting to sue Arthur Scargill and the NUM on behalf of the Conservative government, and imprison him for contempt of court:[7]

---

[7] In a case brought by five miners from Yorkshire and Derbyshire, the High Court found the 1984–5 strike to be unlawful as it had been undertaken without a ballot (Rogers 1984, 1).

> Sir Hector Laing stumped up some cash
> Lord Hanson stumped up more
> they served a writ on Scargill
> on the Labour Conference floor,
>
> A firm of Tory lawyers
> deployed the state machine
> and outlawed Scargill and the NUM
> to the silence of the TUC.
>
> See, all those bastards need to win
> is Brotherhood to fail
> in cringing fear of state assault
> of courts and fines and jail. (Ely 2015, 139)[8]

The TUC's 'silence' is an example of the factions within the trade union movement. As Ely, through machine/TUC, withholds the expected end-rhyme, the TUC has effectively been silenced by the 'state machine' (and by Ely, who sees its voice as unnecessary to tell his labour history) or has chosen to remain silent. The TUC is suspended between the forces of the state and its obligations towards the NUM. The NUM is at the mercy of the 'state', whereas the TUC has the option to remain silent. This silence should be seen in light of the opening of the poem. The NUM removes or withhold its labour—'closing down the cokeworks' (Ely 2015, 138)—to have an impact, the TUC withhold its 'voice'. It is unsurprising then that in the final 22 stanzas of the poem the TUC is not mentioned again, their silence has effectively removed them, at least in the eyes of Ely, from having a role to play in any further history of the miners' dispute.

Unlike the other poets examined, Ely broadens his trade union focus to include two other unions; however, they both appear in the midst of violence. The first appears when Ely is writing about the Northern Irish independence 'troubles' and the latter in regard to the death of the activist Blair Peach at the hands of the police.[9] In 'Irish Blood, English Heart', Ely writes:

---

[8] Sir Hector Laing was Director of the Bank of England in 1984 and Lord Hanson was an industrialist whom Margaret Thatcher made a peer in 1983.

[9] An official report from the Metropolitan police stated that: 'Blair Peach attended a demonstration against a National Front meeting in Southall on the 23rd April 1979. At about 12.10am on the 24th April he died in hospital. Post mortems later showed he died of a head injury. At the time of his death there was a thorough investigation which stated that fourteen witnesses said they saw a police officer hit Blair Peach and that there is no evidence which shows he received the injury in any other way' (Metropolitan Police 2010, n.pag.).

> [...] Mick O'Brien and Kev Malley
> of the Parachute Regiment,
> Derry, Longdon and Belize;
> Dennis Doody of UCATT and the SWP,
> 'unconditional but critical support',
> Patrick Tighe of the NUM
> and South Kirkby Miners' Welfare;
> Joe Connell of Keble
> and the Inns of Court. (2015, 169)

Later, in his poem 'Inglan is a Bitch', Ely writes:

> [...] facing the cop-shop,
> where punk-legend
> 'that' Billy Johnson emulsioned
> THE POLICE KILLED BLAIR
> in square letters three foot high.
> (He'd intended to paint BLAIR *PEACH*,
> but ran out of wall.)
> Blair Peach: teacher,
> activist, man of letters:
> NUT, ANL, SWP. (2015, 179)

The first poem takes its title from the Morrissey song of the same name, in which the singer points to a shared connection between Ireland and England while denouncing British politics and the crown. The second, 'Inglan is a Bitch', takes its title from a Linton Kwesi Johnson song that concerns itself predominantly with the exploitation of manual labour, particularly amongst immigrants. Both poems focus on the state's suppression of opposition and have the unions, UCATT (the Union of Construction, Allied Trades and Technicians) and the NUT (National Union of Teachers), situated alongside the Trotskyist Socialist Workers Party (SWP) and, in the latter case, the Anti-Nazi League (ANL). In the first extract above, both Dennis Doody and Patrick Tighe are defined by their affiliation to a trade union. What is most interesting is that while 'the study of industrial relations is primarily devoted to the relationship between unions and management' (Abercrombie and Warde 1988, 60), in this poem we have the presentation of the relationship between the individual and their union. Yet that relationship is determined only insofar as Doody and Tighe are union members, without establishing what their roles or activities were within that union. In the context of a poem called 'Irish Blood, English Heart', it is impossible not to read the unions Ely cites, and by association Doody and Tighe, in the light of the struggle for Irish independence. Ely has said that the point of the poem is to undermine imperial concepts of 'Great Britain' by affirming and celebrating the Irish struggle for independence whilst at the same time pointing out the paradox is that there is a huge streak of Irishness in the English—and has been for over a thousand years. (personal communication, 13 Jan. 2016)

Through the inclusion of the unions, along with the 'Parachute Regiment' and the 'Inns of Court', Ely is showing this 'streak of Irishness' and how it has come to occupy many of our most influential 'British' institutions. Unions, here, are viewed as organisations that allow 'alternative' voices to be heard and disseminated. These unions exist in a particular intersection between organisational politics and independent activism. Ely's naming of Doody and Tighe, alongside their union affiliation, is essentially synecdochal, refiguring the individual Doody and Tighe as the UCATT and the NUM. This allows them the political 'authority' to speak on issues not generally pertaining to the union itself. The individual can say things that the organisation cannot.

'Inglan is a Bitch' begins with an epigraph composed of lyrics from a Linton Kwesi Johnson song but, oddly, not the song after which the poem is named, rather 'It Dread Inna Inglan (For George Lindo)':[10]

> *Noh mattah wat dey say,*
> *come wat may,*
> *we are here to stay*
> *inna Inglan.* (Ely 2015, 176)

While in 'Irish Blood, English Heart' Ely shows how a 'streak of Irishness' has come to occupy many of our most influential 'British' institutions, the epigraph to 'Inglan' exemplifies how immigration and multiculturalism is an integral part of England and English life. Interestingly for this book, the song 'It Dread Inna Inglan' references Thatcher: 'Maggi Tatcha on di go / Wid a racist show' (Johnson 1978). Thatcher is not mentioned in Ely's poem, nor is the 'bitch' of the poem's title really considered in terms of gender and the representation of women in the poem. In fact, there are very few women in the poem in general. There is a section called 'Mrs Duffy' which defends Gillian Duffy against then PM Gordon Brown's characterisation of her as a 'bigot' after she said, during a televised exchange in 2010, that 'you can't say anything about the immigrants' (Weaver 2010, n.pag.). Yet, on the whole, in the way Ely conceives his 'Inglan', women barely feature.

It is through the figure of Blair Peach that the poem continues the idea, from 'Irish Blood, English Heart', that the individual can say things which

---

[10] George Lindo was wrongly accused of robbing a betting shop in Bradford in 1978.

organisations cannot. Peach was a teacher who was killed by a Special Patrol Group (SPG) police officer while demonstrating against the National Front in 1979. In Ely's poem, the reaction to Peach's death—'Billy Johnson emulsioned / THE POLICE KILLED BLAIR / in square letters three foot high'—precedes the 'obituary' for the man himself, 'Blair Peach: teacher, / activist, man of letters: / NUT, ANL, SWP' (2015, 179). As mentioned in the Introduction, Ely stated that after leaving party politics in 1996 he 'became politically quiescent', commenting that 'I don't count simply "having opinions", even on social media (or in poems), as being politically engaged—you've got to join, campaign, organise, commit, sacrifice' (Ely & Pugh 2015, n.pag.). Blair Peach seems to embody the 'political engagement' to which Ely is referring.

Acronyms necessitate a common vernacular through which to read them, but here it is spelled out for us. We are given a 'key' by which to read them, with 'teacher' reflected in the NUT (National Union of Teachers); 'activist' with ANL (Anti-Nazi League) and, if we are to continue with these counterpoints, 'man of letters' with SWP (Socialist Workers Party). The idea being that without understanding the individual—Peach—we are unable to understand the organisations of which he was a part. While Peach may have been a 'teacher' and 'activist', to simply say or write these things is not engagement enough. It is through the organisational structures that he was a part of—the union, the campaigning group, the political party— that these labels come to have a broader significance and importance. It is through an individual's relationship with institutions that he or she has (greater) political agency. To be a teacher defines you by your labour, but to be part of a union situates you as an agent within the history of the labour movement. Peach being a 'man of letters', through the organisations of which he was a part, means that his death is situated in a much larger social movement. Yet it is the individual to whom 'eight thousand Sikhs / Paid their respects' (Ely 2015, 179), not the organisations of which he was a member. As in 'Irish Blood, English Heart', the individual's organisational position is not what is important. The individual is required as a figure on which to 'affix' a wider, more inclusive (or subversive), public message than the organisation wishes or is able to disseminate. In the poems, Dennis Doody and Blair Peach are given 'validation' by their membership of a trade union and, reciprocally, the unions in the poem are given a 'face' through which, and a figure about which, to speak.

In the poems 'Irish Blood, English Heart' and 'Inglan is a Bitch', UCAAT, the NUM and the NUT are not defined or presented in terms of their relationship to labour itself, but in their relationship to state violence. The narrative that Ely presents situates unions as both victims and bulwarks to state oppression and extremism.

II. Not Unions

To conclude this chapter, the focus will be on one of the most emotive words in trade union circles, 'scab'. Through Helen Mort's *Division Street* (2013) and specifically the poem 'Scab', the focus is on how trade unions can come to be sidelined within strike narratives.

The cover art for *Division Street* is a photograph by Don McPhee taken at the Battle of Orgreave. It shows a picketing miner wearing a homemade police helmet adorned with the badge of the NUM, face to face with a line of police officers.[11] Although the cover introduces us to the NUM, the union does not appear anywhere in Mort's collection. Helen Mort was born in 1985, after the Battle of Orgreave and the 1984–5 miners' strike, at a time when union influence was already waning. When the collection was published, the NUM had, in reality, ceased to be a force in the British trade union movement. However, its involvement in the 1984–5 strike cannot be underplayed.

II.1 Helen Mort's 'Scab'

The strike and its legacy is contended with in the collection's 'centrepiece' poem, 'Scab'—the only poem longer than two pages in the *Division Street*. The five sections move between the legacy of the 1984–5 strike and Mort's time as an undergraduate at the University of Cambridge.

The 'scab' is a figure that reoccurs, also appearing in the title of Ely's 'Ballad of the Scabs'. One of the earliest examples of 'scab' being used to denote a strikebreaker can be found as far back as 1792:

> What is a scab? He is to his *trade* what a traitor is to his *country* [...]
> He first sells the journeymen, and is himself afterwards sold in his turn by the masters, till at last he is despised by both and deserted by all. (Aspinall 1949, 84)

---

[11] 'The Battle of Orgreave', as it has come to be known, took place on 18 June 1984 when miners were 'secondary picketing' at the Orgreave coking plant—picketing at a place, in this case a factory ran by British Steel, that was not directly linked to the protest (McSmith 2011, 163). Estimates put the number of strikers in the region of 10,000 and roughly half that number of police officers (Tarver 2014, n.pag.). According to police reports, '93 pickets were arrested, with a further 51 injured along with 72 police officers' ('IPCC Sorry for Orgreave Probe Delay' 2014, n.pag.). To this day, the Orgreave Truth and Justice Campaign is still pressing the IPCC (Internal Police Complaints Commission) to investigate South Yorkshire Police with regard to the events of that day. In 2015, the IPCC said it would not investigate the police officers in Orgreave that day, as too much time had passed ('"Battle Of Orgreave": Probe into 1984 Miners' Clash Policing Ruled Out' 2016, n.pag.).

The act of 'scabbing' is situated alongside the concept of nationalism or patriotism, essentially equating 'scabbing' with treason. Although this points to the belief in the severity of the 'crime', the quotation also places striking in the same bracket as loyalty to the state or country. Your trade is part of your identity. In 'Ballad of the Scabs', Ely writes, in regard to the Union of Democratic Mineworkers (UDM),[12] that workers should not 'be seduced by bribery' as the 'war is won by unity' and staying true to your 'comrades and your class' (2015, 142). As a worker, you do not work solely for yourself, but in service of your trade, class and all those who are part of it. After selling out the 'journeymen', you will in turn be 'sold [...] by the masters'. Your support comes from your fellow workers, not those in power, however they may seek to convince you otherwise.

In the penultimate stanza of the poem's fifth and final section, Mort writes, '*They scabbed in 1926. They scabbed / in 1974. They'd scab tomorrow / if they had the chance ...*' (2013, 22; emphasis original). The act of scabbing is entwined with industrial disputes, particularly those miners' disputes of 1926, 1974 and 1984–5, in which tens, if not hundreds, of thousands of workers went on strike. We have no specific details about 'who' scabbed, but we have a 'they', the other. The 'they' smooths out strike history; individual choice and social context for these workers to scab is removed or (intentionally) ignored. The 1984–5 strike ended on 3 March 1985. By the end of February 1985, the total number of miners who had abandoned the strike 'exceeded 93,000' of the between 186,000 and 188,000 NUM members (Jones 1986, 184). The 'scabs' made up the majority of the union membership. Yet those who had scabbed—even as far back as 1926—continued to be scabs from that point onwards in the reminiscences of those who had not.

The final phrase, '*They'd scab tomorrow / if they had the chance ...*', seems to combine a lingering anger at those who crossed the picket line with a sorrow that there is no opportunity for anyone to do so again, because of the destruction of the mining industry. By continuing this idea of scabbing, Mort tries to secure a narrative in which these distinctions are still necessary. You can only scab if you are supposed to be on strike, and in most instances strikes only occur with the presence of a (strong) trade union movement. A strike is useless without jobs to protect or working conditions to improve, as are trade unions. Those who 'scabbed' remain a reminder that there had been a trade union and other striking colleagues to undermine.

In Mort's poem, the scab also appears as a wound, the repercussions and marks of the strike yet to disappear. 'Scab' opens by positioning us directly in the midst of the strike:

---

[12] The Union of Democratic Mineworkers (UDM), which was officially established in 1985 (mostly by Nottinghamshire miners who refused to strike, or wished to return to work during the 1984–5 miners' strike), can be considered a 'scab' union.

> A stone is lobbed in '84,
> hangs like a star over Orgreave.
> *Welcome to Sheffield*. Border-land,
> our town of miracles—the wine
> Turning to water in the pubs. (Mort 2013, 16)

Without explaining what happened in 1984, in terms of the strike, or what is or was 'Orgreave', Mort presents these events as indelibly linked to any discussion of Sheffield—enough to constitute a '*Welcome*'. This sets up a division between the poet and reader or, more specifically, those who come from former mining communities and those who have not lived (directly) with the legacy of the strike of 1984–5. In the poem, 1984 *is* the strike and the Battle of Orgreave; no more explanation is needed. Opening the poem with 'is lobbed' presents not just the violence of the event, but also the contemporary ramifications of it. We are given no agent who 'lobbed' the stone, it is either irrelevant or the name is lost to history. Only their actions are remembered. The legacy of 1984 remains, not the names of those involved. There is no specific target, just a general direction, and everyone is a potential victim. With no thrower or intended victim, Mort leaves the stone suspended in mid-air, never reaching the ground but shining down 'over Orgreave', until the poem's close. This is a place where time has stood still, the action of the strike arresting any forward movement, yet at the same time 'illuminating' everything that has come since, and proving a fitting introduction to Sheffield.

The single star over Orgreave brings to mind either the Pole Star or the star of Bethlehem, signifying the birth of Christ. The stone and Orgreave become a focal point around which people can rally. Orgreave and the protest come to symbolise something bigger than the 1984–5 strike itself. If we push the Bible story further, it is the 'wise men' who, after seeing the star, report it to Herod. Herod then calls for the execution of all the male babies in Bethlehem, so as to prevent the loss of his throne. Transposing this reading to the poem, the stone/star becomes not only a rallying point, but also that which causes untold suffering for years to come. The closure of the mines led to the destruction and deprivation of mining communities and a lack of jobs for future generations—'at the onset of the strike, the NCB [National Coal Board] employed a workforce of 208,000 [...] Within ten years, more than 90 per cent of the jobs were gone' (McSmith 2011, 169). Herod's 'massacre of the innocents' is about the threat of new leadership and the attempt to negate future challenges to his power. That negation, however, is achieved by ordering the killing of male children; females are spared. It is a story that says women are not a challenge to power. In fact, it is a story that doesn't really consider women at all. While this could be taken as a comment on strike history's neglect of the stories of women, Mort is sustaining a dynamic that sidelines the role women played in strike histories. This is perhaps unfair on Mort in that, as the only female poet in this book and writing about strike histories, she is herself part of a pushback that says women can tell strike histories, and tell them in a way that pertains to them. Mort's work is still in conversation with all the male-dominated strike narratives that have come before (and still predominate now), yet at least we have a different perspective on these stories.

Thatcher's destruction of the mining industry should be read in the same way as the Massacre of the Innocents, as an attempt to preserve political power at any cost. If you destroy an industry, you inevitably destroy the union that represents it (and, as a consequence, those who are represented by it). In light of this, '*Welcome to Sheffield*' takes on a far more demoralising resonance, Sheffield being a place unable to forget or move on, a city in a state of arrested development where 'miracles' consist of 'wine / turning to water in the pubs' (Mort 2013, 16). Jen Harvie states that 'remembering can be a progressive or regressive political act' (2005, 41); here, remembering is being used to show how development has not simply been arrested but is actively regressing. The legacy of the strike continues, but development does not.

'Scab' ends with the stone from the poem's opening finally crashing through 'your windowpane', where the 'you' is 'left / to guess which picket line you crossed':

> One day, it crashes through
> your windowpane, the stone,
> the word, the fallen star. You're left
> to guess which picket line
> you crossed—a gilded College gate,
> a better supermarket, the entrance
> to your flat where, even now, someone
> has scrawled the worst insult they can—
> a name. Look close. It's yours. (Mort 2013, 22–3)

The past comes crashing into the present of the poem, destroying the view of the strike that had been created, challenged and undermined through various recollections and reconstructions of the strike, and through the refashioning of these events as a poem. As Seumas Milne states, 'far from being remote from our time, the miners' opposition to Thatcher's market and privatization juggernaut makes even clearer sense in the wake of the 2008 crash than it did at the time' (2014, 397). Both the reader and Mort become the 'scab' of the poem's title. The 'you' is left to 'guess' which picket line was crossed; the arbitrary nature of the guess implying that all of us have in some fashion 'crossed the picket line', without being fully aware of it. These crossed borders—'a gilded College gate / a better supermarket, the entrance to your flat' (Mort 2013, 23)—speak to the feeling in the 1980s that 'no longer was being working class something to be proud of: it was something to escape from' (Jones 2012, 40). We are now becoming, or have become, products of the strike's legacy. In the same way that Harrison's work is concerned with leaving behind his 'heritage', Mort brings the same concerns bursting into the twenty-first century and ends the poem with another allusion to Harrison: 'someone / has scrawled the worst insult they can— / a name. Look close. It's yours' (Mort 2013, 23). The 'look close' conjures the image of someone straining to read a name that, while theirs, has become unfamiliar to them. As earlier in the poem where a re-enactor is kicked until 'he doesn't know his name' (Mort 2013, 19), here the name is never given to us and in that space it becomes that of the reader. The poem breaks through the 'windowpane' which positions the reader as an observer, and repositions the reader as both the subject and the object of the poem. The reader becomes the 'you' who has crossed the picket line and the 'scrawled' name becomes the reader's own. The reader is exposed as (unintentionally) complicit in the continuation and dissemination of these strike narratives. The legacy of the miners' strike is so pervasive that there is no 'you' (reading the poem) that is exempt from its influence and legacy.

This concern with names continues in the 'third section' of the poem, where Mort's focus turns to one of the most unusual works created in response to the miners' strike of 1984–5, artist Jeremy Deller's 2001 re-enactment of the Battle of Orgreave. The re-enactment featured 'eight hundred people, many of whom were ex-miners or police involved in the original encounter' (Mort 2013, n.pag.).

The section opens by informing us that what we are reading is not real, that this poem, along with the reconstruction it recounts, is part of the attempt to fashion and reform these strike narratives:

> This is a reconstruction. Nobody
> will get hurt. There are miners playing
> coppers, ex-coppers shouting
> *Maggie, Out.* There are battle specialists. (Mort 2013, 19)

The opening line serves as a warning to the reader of what is to come and a reminder to (us and) those taking part that this is not a 'real' battle. In the next two verses, there is also a shift in the opening lines from 'reconstruction' to 're-enactment' and back again: you 'reconstruct' the narrative, then you 're-enact' this past narrative, before reconstructing a new narrative based on this re-enactment. Narratives are shaped by narratives. In her work on site-specific performance, Jen Harvie asserts that:

> Site-specific performance can enact a spatial history, mediating
> between the past and the present most obviously, but also between

> the identities of the past and those of the present and future, as well as between a sense of nostalgia for the past and a sense of otherness possibly felt in the present and anticipated in the future. (2005, 42)

Despite Harvie's contention, any reconstruction or performance enacting this type of 'spatial history'—particularly of an event such as the Battle of Orgreave—will always be influenced by the material it is based on (and the person organising the reconstruction). These 'identities' Harvie writes of are still subject to the person creating the performance. In Mort's poem, the 'reconstruction' is immediately undermined by the assertion that 'nobody will get hurt' and the fact that in some cases the miners and 'coppers' who were involved will be playing the 'parts' of one another. Mort is demonstrating a process whereby 'history' becomes reduced to a staged presentation of reportedly 'true' events. As Richard Schechner, by way of Baudrillard, comments, if 'the simulation can seem real, the opposite is also true—the real can appear to be simulated' (2006, 138). Not only does Schechner's idea speak to the event Mort is commenting upon, but also to the poem itself. The poem is a poetic 'reconstruction' of an event which was itself a reconstruction of a previous event. Through the performative action of the 'reconstruction' and through Mort's own work, we are constantly being made aware of the way that accounts of an event can shift, be appropriated and be reconstructed—to build something again, but not necessarily in the way that it once was. Once narratives are retold and reconstructed to the extent that these reconstructions and appropriations become the dominant view of an event, it is almost impossible to re-establish the 'real', if such a thing ever existed. The 'real' is simply part of the reconstruction. In the initial reconstruction, parts are assigned depending on the needs of the performance; in Mort's work, they are assigned according to the 'needs' of the poem.

However, a reconstruction is not necessarily an inferior copy of the original; it is 'neither a pretense nor an imitation. It is a replication of [...] itself as another' (Schechner 2006, 117). Both Mort's poem and Deller's reconstruction are original pieces of work, and original pieces which omit trade unions. As Mort's work draws directly from Deller's re-enactment for the poem, as opposed to the 'real' Battle of Orgreave, it shows the way that myths and narratives can be created and disseminated and how they can be appropriated to fill a particular need or narrative. Mort has chosen to use Deller's staged and documented event as her starting point, rather than the memories of miners involved in the original event, showing the arbitrary fashion by which histories can be constructed. One of the most telling lines is that where Mort writes, 'This is a reconstruction. / It is important to film everything' (2013, 20). The reconstruction of the event was a single, site-specific performance, while the need to 'film everything' shifts the temporary into something more permanent. As the mainstream media at the time of the strike 'mostly portrayed the strike as an anti-democratic insurrection that defied economic logic' (Milne 2014, xii), the desire to capture the reconstruction on film can be viewed as a way of redressing the anti-miner narrative of the media version of the strike.[13] Yet there is a sense that the doctored image presented by the media is being replaced by another stylised view of the struggle. As Alan Sinfield comments, it is 'the contest between rival stories [that] produces our notions of reality' (2007, 26–7). As a great deal of the Battle of Orgreave was not filmed, the re-enactment, which by being filmed passes into something approaching permanence, becomes another 'official' version of events. The re-enactment and Mort's poem add to and complicate the 'canon' of the miners' strike legacy.

Mort's poem is accessing that media—or, at least, the documentation of the reconstruction—but seemingly questioning what it is that is being retained by it. What Mort has retained in the poem are the figures of the 'battle specialists', the new authority figures giving instructions during the re-enactment and the performative aspects of the 'language used for authenticity' (2013, 19). These 'battle specialists' come to shape the narrative and control how the story is told. The original miners involved in the battle, however, have been marginalised. Harvie states that site-specific performance 'may validate identities that have been historically marginalised or oppressed, and they may revise potential imbalances in the power dynamics between communities' (2005, 41). In the poem, the identities are in part invalidated by the switching of 'roles' with 'miners playing / coppers' and 'ex-coppers shouting / *Maggie, Out*' (Mort 2012, 19). To swap roles suggests that there is no validity in your original role, just in the role you are assigned for the performance. The story you are telling and the performance must have the appearance of truth, even if it does not reflect reality.

Whether miner or police officer, all are caught up in the legacy of the miners' strike. If roles are assigned regardless of the participants' original

---

[13] Famously, BBC news edited the film from Orgreave so that it appeared that the miners had attacked the police, not vice versa as was the case. In its 'eagerness to select and shape events to fit a pre-formulated interpretation', the BBC 'missed by a mile what was to become the main story of Orgreave' (Masterman 1984, 105). In the BBC's report, 'the violence at Orgreave was presented unequivocally as picket violence […] with picketing turning to rioting and destruction and the police compelled to act defensively to retain control under tremendous pressure' (Masterman 1984, 101–2). However, ITN's footage showed that the decision to '"turn nasty" was one deliberately made by the police. The film showed the police lines opening up, the horses galloping into a group of pickets, who were simply standing around, and the riot police following up wielding their truncheons' (Masterman 1984, 102).

job, the suggestion is that they could have been on the other 'side' at Orgreave. David Griffiths, a miner at the Taff Merthyr Colliery in Wales, recalled that during the strike 'more and more police were drafted in and even though the government strongly denied it, many miners believe the army were also on the picket line. I saw it with my own eyes, a miner on a picket line with me spotted his own son, who was supposedly in the army fighting for his country [...] this man would never speak to his son again' (Butts-Thompson 2014, 22). At one time, these types of jobs offered security and a reasonable wage for many. Harrison's 'class v. class' (2008, 11) can be seen playing out here; the other 'class' was not necessarily from a different economic and social background, but a different version of yourself or your family, a version who joined the police force rather than going down the mines.

Towards the end of the 'reconstruction', a re-enactor is told to kick another 'till he doesn't know his name'. We are presented with a tension between the assertion that 'nobody will get hurt' and this overt encouragement of violence. If the re-enactor is instructed to kick the person until 'he doesn't know his name', there is the implication that there is some value within a name. Yet we do not know, and are never given, the name of the re-enactor, or the role they are supposed to be playing. We are, ironically, being told to forget something that we have never known. Mort here is highlighting the gaps in our histories and the ways in which the individual can become lost in service of a broader narrative. There is a questioning of the attention afforded to the violence at Orgreave, rather than those involved in the action. The section of the poem ends with two miners hiding 'beneath the bed', not sure if they are 'lost' or 'left for dead' by the re-enactment, by the poem and by the system that forced them out of work in the first place without adequate support (Mort 2013, 20). While the poem brings to light issues surrounding the event itself (Orgreave and the strike) and perhaps attempts to revise potential 'imbalances in the power dynamics' of these narratives (Erll 2011, 41), Mort is showing the way in which alternative voices and figures come to be excluded from our narratives. These miners taking part in the reconstruction become complicit in continuing and reinforcing a narrative that seeks to silence them.

The poems in this chapter show the tension between the collective and the individual in our labour narratives. They demonstrate the ways in which collectives can both obscure individual voices and yet require them to humanise our strike histories. Both MacSweeney and Ely assert the complicity between the TUC and the state, the TUC undermining union action through 'closed door pacts' with the government or by remaining conspicuously silent. In O'Brien, the figure of a striker is inserted into the poem before being sidelined by the 'official' strike narrative. Harrison and Mort warn about seeing labour narratives as existing within narrowly delineated boundaries, while exposing them as artful constructions. All these poems see our strike narratives as a negotiation. They are a negotiation between those groups that endeavour to control the narratives and those who attempt to contest them. However, what is clear is that these positions are not absolute. In these narratives, how we position ourselves (and are positioned by others) is part of the construction.

CHAPTER THREE

Naming Scargills and Thatchers

> 'My name is Alice, but—'
> 'It's a stupid name enough!' Humpty Dumpty interrupted impatiently. 'What does it mean?'
> 'Must a name mean something?' Alice asked doubtfully.
> 'Of course it must,' Humpty Dumpty said with a short laugh: 'my name means the shape I am—and a good handsome shape it is, too. With a name like yours, you might be any shape, almost.'
>
>   Lewis Carroll, *Alice Through the Looking Glass* (1866)

This chapter explores constructions of the individual, in particular Arthur Scargill and Margaret Thatcher, two figures whose legacy looms large over any discussion of late twentieth-century trade unionism in the UK. The focus here is on the politics of naming—with attention paid to how Arthur Scargill and, to a lesser extent, Margaret Thatcher are 'constructed' through these acts of naming. In regard to strike narratives, these acts of naming come to work as a form of cultural dominion and/or opposition.

In the 1985 essay 'Mining the Meaning: Key Words in the Miners' Strike', Raymond Williams wrote that 'in the coal strike, there are central issues of great importance to the society, but around them, and often obscuring them, the noise and dust and stone of confused, short-term or malignant argument' (1989b, 120). Williams defined these 'central issues' under the four keywords: '*management; economic; community*; and *law and order*'. He saw these keywords as underpinning the way in which the future of society 'would come to be decided' (1989b, 120). Williams is speaking to the potential legacies of the 1984–5 miners' strike and his concerns that these legacies would come to frame the strike as an almost malevolent act. Even while the strike was happening, Williams was aware of the dangers of the narrative being co-opted or misrepresented. Williams said that 'it is of the lasting honour of the miners, and the women, and the old people, and all the others in the defiant communities, that they have stood up against [...] and challenged' a capitalism that 'exploits actual places and people' (1989b, 124). While these groups stood against those who sought to close the mines, they were unable to control the strike's legacy.

Lizzie and John Eldridge, in their book on Williams, *Making Connections*, write that 'the purpose of the article was not to make judgements on the tactics, timing or personalities of the strike' (2004, n.pag.). Scargill is not really present in Williams's essay. He is there by implication only, as the figure who called the strike and brought it into being.[1] Yet Scargill's actions during the miners' strike of 1984–5 are undoubtedly caught up in the concerns that Williams writes about. Fred Inglis writes of Scargill being 'a self-righteous class warrior of passionate feeling and few wits but who had got hold of the truth that the class enemy was always a ruthless liar' (1998, 281). This concern with truth and lies suggests that the battle over narratives is itself caught up in a broader class politics. The enemies of the working class are those who control the dominant narrative, those who seek to exclude the voices which attempt to challenge it. For Williams, the key to understanding how narratives are formed and controlled is through the 'dynamic interrelations' between 'residual, emergent and dominant' cultural forms and processes (1977, 121).

'Residual' cultural processes are those that, while being formed in the past, are still an active and 'effective element' of contemporary cultural processes, but are not the dominant element. An illustrative example of the complexity of such relations is that of the 'rural community':

> The idea of the rural community is predominantly residual, but is in some limited respects alternative or oppositional to urban industrial capitalism, though for the most part it is incorporated, as idealization or fantasy, or as an exotic—residential or escape—leisure function of the dominant order itself. (Williams 1977, 122)

Residual processes can be oppositional. The continuation of residual cultural processes can also be as a result of their incorporation into 'effective dominant cultures'. It is not simply that the 'residual' is 'incorporated' into a dominant culture, but how this incorporated process is then made to function that is important. Williams uses the phrase 'idealization or

---

[1] Although Williams never wrote directly about Scargill, his 1985 novel *Loyalties*, which begins in 1936 with the rise of fascism in the UK and ends at the close of 1984 in the midst of the miners' strike (yet still does not mention Scargill at all), was sent by Andrew Motion, who worked for the publisher Chatto & Windus at the time, 'to, among others, Neil Kinnock, Arthur Scargill' (Inglis 1998, 282). There is nothing to say whether Scargill received the novel, let alone read it.

fantasy' to demonstrate the way in which the incorporated processes are refashioned as 'other'. Refashioning seeks to discredit residual cultural narratives by positioning them as 'fantasy'—a part of culture that is either impossible to retrieve or never actually existed. However, when incorporation does occur, it is always selective. The dominant is able to choose from these residual processes, with the overarching aim of maintaining the dominant.

The incorporation of cultural processes that could become oppositional, or are actively outside the dominant, is managed through 'reinterpretation, dilution, projection' and 'discriminating inclusion and exclusion', which limits any potential threat to the hegemonic structure by making these processes part of the dominant (Williams 1977, 123). It is through this selective incorporation that the dominant attempts to control 'emergent' cultural forms. Emergent forms are those 'new meanings and values, new practices, new relationships and kinds of relationship' that are constantly being constructed (Williams 1977, 122).

The difficulty with emergent forms, according to Williams, is the ability to distinguish those which are truly emergent and contribute to alternative or oppositional cultural processes and those which appear emergent but are simply new manifestations of the dominant (1977, 123). This is also true of our narratives and histories. Are our 'alternative voices' truly contesting how we see our histories, or are they themselves simply a contribution to those already dominant narratives? It is those practices which are truly emergent and thereby oppositional to the hegemony that are most at risk of incorporation, because it is those emergent practices that highlight the hegemony's lack of absolute control. For Williams, the 'residual' and the 'emergent' are as important as the 'dominant', for it is they that reveal 'the characteristics of the "dominant"' (1977, 122). Pushing Williams's point further, not only do the emergent and the residual reveal the characteristics of the dominant, they can also reveal its particular and shifting fears.

With this chapter I contend that through acts of naming and renaming these 'strike' poems demonstrate the ways in which dominant cultural forms attempt to assume (and subsume) residual and emergent cultural modes while those modes, in turn, attempt to resist such dominion. The final lines of Tony Harrison's 'Them & [uz]' exemplifies this idea more succinctly than I can: 'My first mention in the *Times* / automatically made Tony Anthony' (1995, 34). Who makes our names and what do we (and others) make of them?

I. Naming

When it comes to naming in the poems, particularly in reference to real figures, how we come to judge and read these names inevitably shifts, depending on the circumstances in which the name is produced (and received). While, for example, 'Mr Scargill', 'Scargill' and 'Arthur Scargill' refer to the same object, these objects are constructed and conceived differently in each iteration. In Theodore Sider's development of Kripke's 'rigid designators', Sider asserts that 'a proper name denotes different objects relative to different times' (2001, 193). In truth, a proper name denotes different objects relative to different times, places and media. Highlighting the forms and places in which names 'exist' allows us to more effectively examine both the situation in which the name is constructed and the situation in which the name is 'received', and the dynamic between these two states. A proper name does not just denote different objects relative to different times, the name is itself a different object.

With specific reference to literature, Alastair Fowler writes that 'literary names are not inherited: they must be found or invented. And writers find it hard to find the right name, one that relinquishes shadowy alternatives and embraces a definite character' (2008, 99). The 'characters' in these strike poems have names (and characters) which are both invented and inherited. They are inherited in so much as, for instance, Scargill and Thatcher have already acquired names—those given to them at birth—and invented in that names—King Arthur, Mr Scargill—are constructed (and presented) in such a way as to induce, expose or further a particular cultural narrative.

*

In the poems that reference the NUM, one of the most commonly bestowed titles on Arthur Scargill is the altogether rather bombastic, yet often tongue-in-cheek, 'King Arthur'.

I.I Paul Bentley's 'The Two Magicians'
Paul Bentley's 'The Two Magicians', from 2011's *Largo*, has as its focus the 1984–5 miners' strike, but situates memories of the strike within the apparently nostalgic context of the poet's teenage years. Of the poem itself Bentley has said that: 'I thought of this poem as a poem of voices – a patchwork of direct quotations, memories, and echoes, stitched loosely onto the old ballad' (Bentley n.d.). In *Memory in Oral Tradition*, when talking about traditional ballads, David Rubin claims that formally the 'general properties, or constraints' of the ballad 'remain stable' and that unlike the traditional epic, the 'exact words change more slowly' (1995, 5). Bentley's 'old ballad' points towards the poem being a work of, or at least inspired by, an oral tradition where the original authorship of the ballad becomes less important than the continuation of the story itself. In terms of strike narratives, it is the legacy that is of note, not who constructed it.

In a review of *Largo*, Matthew Stewart homes in on Bentley's use of 'high' and 'low' cultural references: 'The miners all coming out at midnight. / Kev Robinson's sister going to bed. / Porphyro stealing along at midnight' (Bentley 2011, 8). Stewart highlights the fact that '"Kev" and "steal" (in this semantic context) are contrasting registers, and the effect is forced home by the allusions to miners and Porphyro in a single stanza' (2012, n.pag.). Bentley's work is an amalgam of registers and layers of cultural appropriation. He is situating his personal memories of the strike, alongside a reference to Keats's 'The Eve of St. Agnes', to establish a space for the poem and to present the patchwork and constructed nature of our strike narratives and legacies.

It is within this context of mixed registers and cultural reference points that 'King Arthur' is introduced:

> King Arthur striking the table
>   harder, raving and growing more fierce and wild.
> New Order: Because we're rebels.
>   Talks breaking down. O bide, lady, bide.
> Johnny Marr's guitar screaming, echoing—
> Mum's *Turn that down I can't hear myself think!*
> Two boys on top of the pile, picking coal.
>   Me thoughts I heard one calling: Child. (Bentley 2011, 12)

Here, Bentley presents us with a range of (pop) cultural reference points. 'King Arthur' is an obvious reference to Arthur Scargill, and a nickname used by his supporters and detractors alike, which situates Scargill as a 'character' from legend as well as connecting the poem to popular cultural parlance of the mid-1980s. Alongside 'King Arthur', the 'table' becomes that which seated the legendary Knights of the Round Table. 'O bide, lady, bide' comes from an old British folk song, 'The Two Magicians', from which Bentley's poem takes its name. The song tells the story of a woman trying to fend off the advances of a 'coal black-smith'.[2] The first, second and final lines are lifted almost verbatim from the seventeenth-century poet George Herbert's 'The Collar' (1633). Finally, New Order is a rock band formed in the 1980s and Johnny Marr was lead guitarist in The Smiths, both bands originating from Manchester. The work is a palimpsest of poems, myths, histories and pop culture. All of these things are part of Bentley's strike narrative.

Of particular interest here is Bentley's attempt to, after a fashion, write Arthur Scargill into Herbert's poem. Herbert's 'The Collar' opens with the line, 'I struck the board, and cried, "No more"' (2005, 379). The cry is uttered by the 'collared' protagonist of the poem wishing to unbind

---

[2] 'I'd rather I were dead and cold / And my body laid in grave / Ere a rusty stock o' coal-black-smith, / My maidenhead should have' (Buchan 1875, 25).

himself, at least temporarily, from that which would control him. The final four lines of Herbert's poem are also reimagined by Bentley:

> But as I raved and grew more fierce and wild
>   At every word
> Methought I heard one calling, *Child!*
>   And I replied *My Lord*. (Herbert 2005, 379)

By equating Scargill with or casting him as the choleric figure from Herbert's poem, Bentley situates him within a broader canon of literary figures and histories. We have Arthur Scargill no longer as a union figurehead, but as part of the cultural milieu of the poem. Bentley untethers Scargill from a union-based environment; even if the use of 'to strike' is a less than subtle link to the miners' struggle and Scargill's involvement in it. With 'King Arthur', Bentley elevates Scargill to the position occupied by one of the UK's most omnipresent legends. Here, the myth and the figure are entwined, and Arthur Scargill cannot escape the idea of 'King Arthur'. It is an idea that suggests power but, as in the Raymond Williams quotation earlier in the chapter, it is an idea which involves a degree of incorporation that turns Scargill into an 'idealization or fantasy' that removes his political efficacy (Williams 1977, 122). As fantasy or idealisation, Scargill poses significantly less of a threat. Bentley is destabilizing notions of authority and foregrounding questions regarding narrative and legacy.

As 'King Arthur' within the Herbert poem, Arthur Scargill as a 'historical' figure becomes buried further beneath, or must bear the weight of, Bentley's range of reference points. The final 'my lord' of Herbert's poem points towards the character's acceptance of authority, or a lessening of his opposition to authority. Bentley links the finally acceptant figure in 'The Collar' with himself, as the person who thought he 'heard one calling: Child'. Bentley 'withholds' the final line of 'The Collar' from his poem, leaving Scargill 'fierce' and 'wild', but tempered by the wild/Child rhyme. The 'memories' of Scargill are as one 'fierce and wild', but those are the remembrances of a 'child'.

In 'The Two Magicians', Scargill never reaches a point of acceptance. Our reading is haunted by the acceptance from the omitted final line of 'The Collar'—'And I replied *My Lord*'—which the Scargill of the poem never receives. Bentley's strike narrative, by its nature, is constructed so as to give significance to certain aspects that Bentley has selected, while obscuring other elements. Bentley reveals to us his workings, yet leaves it to us to give attention to them. Bentley foregrounds his selection process for his (particular) strike narrative. The space that Bentley's selection creates and the alternative cultural products that he invokes, regardless of his intention, demonstrates the impossibility of attempting to effectively silence counter-narratives. Bentley brings onto the stage of the poem a collection of images and associations to present a cross-section of the influences that make up his strike memories. They exist together in the same 'moment', the 'stories' working with and competing against one another for dominance.

As Benjamin Kunkel writes in *Utopia or Bust*, 'a basic feature of dialectical thinking is the liability of subject and object to turn into each other, for a way a thing is looked at to become part of the look of a thing [...] Does a statue confirm the living influence of a man, or only that he belongs in the past?' (2014, 58). This is the question Bentley poses with 'King Arthur'. Does the idea of Arthur Scargill survive on its own or is he being propped up by the poem itself? The answer could be the first: Scargill is being written about by Bentley because his legacy exists, or at least Bentley believes in the legacy. However, this legacy is now tied up in so much narrative, counter-narrative and cultural 'bleed' that it is impossible to separate the man from the cultural products in which he is represented. The narratives and legacies themselves are contributing to the construction of Scargill.

I.II Barry MacSweeney's 'John Bunyan to Johnny Rotten'
It is not only Bentley, writing in 2011, who plays with the image and myth of Arthur Scargill. Barry MacSweeney's 1997 poem 'John Bunyan to Johnny Rotten', from *Book of Demons*, is described by W.N. Herbert as 'a type of psychic journey from the state of mind of the Pilgrim to that of John Lydon' (2013, 155). The poem opens on 'long shadows of gold October' and 'amber crowns of trees' before journeying towards the nihilistic, 'no rain on the gravel or mist in the hair / can save us from the eternal prospekt of the knacker's yard' and ending with a Sex Pistols inspired shout of '¡GOD SAVE THE / QUEEN!' (MacSweeney 2003, 284, 289, 290). It is a journey in which Arthur Scargill plays a (relatively minor) role. Yet it is a poem which frames Scargill in a fashion not dissimilar from his presentation in Bentley's 'The Two Magicians'.

MacSweeney's 'King Arthur' is 'consumed' by another cultural reference point, in this instance the nursery rhyme 'Sing a Song of Sixpence':

Tom, King Arthur's in his counting house, counting out the wastage,
finalising the blame,
And who would say it, Thomas, who would lift the gall from the cracked glass,
but to say: Arthur, you too were a croupier of blame, you too
Swept the table clean with the other social model, Margaret of St. Francis?
(2003, 286)

In MacSweeney's poem, Arthur Scargill is not simply the 'King Arthur' of Arthurian legend, but the king from 'Sing a Song of Sixpence'. The nursery rhyme MacSweeney employs is much more recognisable than 'The Collar' used by Bentley. After we identify the nursery rhyme, our expectations precede our reading of the line; we expect the word 'money', but we are forced to recalibrate. We expect 'money', we find 'wastage'. There is no money left and this strike narrative is one of waste and loss. 'Wastage' is the dismantling of a mining industry (and the communities built to serve it), the decline of the trade union movement, the loss of Scargill's own power and the lost wages of the miners.

The title 'King' takes on a quality of failure, as one who has status or is perceived to have power and influence, but being without funds—here both monetary and in terms of influence—only a title is left. MacSweeney's use of the term 'King' is not mockery, but rather it highlights the creation of a symbol. This symbol is of a figure (Scargill) unable to disengage themselves from the past, or be disengaged from the stories surrounding their past. MacSweeney's use of 'finalising', with its emphasis on something nearing, but never reaching, an end, leaves Scargill looking to attribute blame but never finding someone to attribute it to. The implication is that Scargill is unwilling to hold himself accountable for any of the failures of the miners' strike of 1984–5. In the poem, Scargill is locked within a myth that is driving his legacy. Yet, in the end, this legacy is partly of our own making.

MacSweeney's shift from 'King Arthur' to 'Arthur' is precipitated by an implied shift in the relationship of the imagined 'speaker' to Arthur Scargill: the use of the Christian name conveying the impression of a (semi-)personal relationship between speaker and recipient. What we are also presented with is a 'dethroning' of King Arthur. The 'legend' is removed. Similarly, MacSweeney shifts 'Tom' to 'Thomas', a reverse in the direction of formality witnessed by the move from 'King Arthur' to 'Arthur'. The speaker is both talking to 'Tom', who becomes 'Thomas', as well as revealing a power dynamic through the act of naming and renaming. These acts of naming expose the tension between public—'Thomas'—and private—'Tom'—representations of Scargill. It is 'Tom' who is aligned with 'King Arthur' and 'Thomas' who is aligned with 'Arthur', the private 'Scargill'. MacSweeney presents a relational quality between the two (or four) figures of Scargill and Thomas in which the negotiation between the public and the private representations of both 'characters', and their relationship to the other character in this negotiation, is continuously being reimagined and repositioned. What this negotiation does is place Scargill within the realms of a 'residual culture'. Raymond Williams writes that a residual culture is one that 'has effectively been formed in the past, but it is still active in the cultural process' (1977, 122). Scargill is still present in the construction of our labour narratives, and therefore 'active' in the cultural process, but he is no longer a 'threat' to the culturally 'dominant' present.

The interesting facet of residual culture is that it contains elements that may 'have an alternative or even oppositional relation to the dominant culture' as well as elements that have 'been wholly or largely incorporated into the dominant culture' (Williams 1977, 122). In these cultural terms, Scargill as 'King Arthur' encompasses elements of the 'dominant' and the 'oppositional'. In terms of the 'dominant', 'King' acts as a reference to the monarchy and a representative of cultural dominion. As 'oppositional', Scargill is referred to as monarch yet occupies a cultural position outside of the ruling classes. MacSweeney presents a shift whereby this move from 'King Arthur' to 'Arthur' reconsiders the role that Scargill occupies. In 1997, when the poem was published, Scargill had very little real political efficacy.[3] The dominant and oppositional elements of Scargill evinced by 'King' are stripped away. It is not so much that Scargill becomes 'incorporated' into a dominant mode or mollified as Arthur, but that he has slipped (or is slipping) towards cultural irrelevance. There is no requirement to incorporate something that is no longer a threat. As 'King Arthur', Scargill has a public profile and a cultural history, as 'Arthur' he has none. In this reading, the contrast between 'Arthur' and 'Margaret of St Francis' becomes even more stark.

'Margaret of St Francis' seems to be an amalgam of Margaret Thatcher and Francis of Assisi (1182–1226). When Margaret Thatcher became Prime Minister on 4 May 1979 she read from a prayer which has often been attributed to Francis of Assisi: 'Where there is discord, may we bring harmony. Where there is error, may we bring truth. Where there is doubt, may we bring faith. And where there is despair, may we bring hope' ('Remarks on Becoming Prime Minister (St Francis' Prayer)'). In 1997, when 'John Bunyan to Johnny Rotten' was published, Thatcher had been out of office for seven years. A Conservative government led by John Major held power in Parliament, while Tony Blair's (New) Labour would soon become the majority party. Although many reading the poem would be familiar with Thatcher's quoting of Assisi, what MacSweeney is doing is re-presenting a part of cultural history that has been obscured by the events of Thatcher's premiership. MacSweeney is foregrounding this cultural history through his reference to St Francis, but also veiling it by withholding the direct relationship between Thatcher and Assisi. As someone who referred to Thatcher derogatorily as a 'stainless bint' in the poem 'Colonel B' (2003, 92), MacSweeney's 'Margaret of St Francis' is undoubtedly critical.

Looking at the phrase 'the other social model', in light of the readings of 'Arthur' and 'Margaret of St Francis', MacSweeney is questioning the way authority is presented. By situating Thatcher as 'the other social model', Scargill being the first, MacSweeney presents us with the only

---

[3] Scargill's Socialist Labour Party received only 0.2 per cent of the national vote in the 1997 General Election (Morgan 1997).

two 'models' to which we can subscribe. There is no room for ambiguity about your political affiliation, you are either Scargill or Thatcher, and modelled as such. MacSweeney uses the image of 'the cracked glass' to position Scargill and Thatcher as reflections of one another that have come to reject or refuse their similarities. Each side 'supports' the other. Scargill and Thatcher are integral to the cultural continuation of the other. Both Scargill and Thatcher are partly constructed through (and limited by) their relation to the other.

Yet there is another argument to be made that through the modification of names we witness a Scargill who requires Thatcher for his own legacy more than Thatcher's legacy relies on Scargill. The shift from 'King' to 'Arthur' shows a waning of influence, with Scargill's position being reduced until it is secured by the introduction of 'Margaret of St Francis', albeit with Scargill now in a subservient position. Thatcher's appearance in the poem ends the verse and explicitly positions Scargill in relation to her. It is Thatcher who is given the final say. The spectre of Thatcher that inevitably hangs behind any discussion of Arthur Scargill is realised and 'Arthur' is enveloped by Thatcher, never to be mentioned again in the poem.

MacSweeney highlights the performativity of the poem and that of the cultural history that it draws from and contributes to, in a form not dissimilar to Bentley in 'The Two Magicians'. The references that MacSweeney embeds within his poem show the issues inherent when labour histories emerge, and the struggles of contending with already established narratives: how are they shaped and how do they shape our understanding? Through the act of naming in the poem, MacSweeney is constantly fashioning and shaping our responses to Scargill and Thatcher, even while telling us that what we are reading is itself a selective history. MacSweeney presents our labour narratives as constructions. These are narratives that have only the appearance of inevitability.

I.III Sean O'Brien's 'Unregistered'

O'Brien's *The Frighteners* (1987) includes a number of poems that allude to the miners' strike of 1984–5, although only the poem 'Unregistered' directly mentions Arthur Scargill. However, O'Brien does not refer to him by his full name, or even by his surname, nor by the laudatory (and/or ironic) 'King Arthur', but with the altogether more reserved title of 'Mr Scargill'.

In 'Unregistered', O'Brien explores how dominant forces seek to control our access to information and, as a result, shape our narratives. The poem recounts the plan by the Conservative government, originally outlined in 1977's leaked Ridley Report and instigated during the 1984–5 strike, to import foreign coal with the intended effect of undermining the NUM's efforts to halt the movement of coal around the UK.[4] These unregistered ports and their unregistered cargo is from where the poem's title comes. The title plays on notions of authority, the power of the 'official', but also the power of absence. In all circumstances, acts of registration are performed by someone in a position of authority. The title of the poem echoes the view behind the final two lines of O'Brien's 'Summertime'—also from *The Frighteners*—where he writes, '*That kind of thing can't happen here / And when it does it isn't true*' (1987, 18). During the strike, there was officially no coal being imported into the UK. This was untrue. At Glasson dock, Lancashire, 'coal boats docked on every tide from East Germany and Poland, to be unloaded directly onto lorries queueing at the dock gates' (Winterton and Winterton 1989, 92).

Each of the poem's four stanzas opens with the phrase 'Six Cranes'. Yet it is not until the final stanza that the purpose of the cranes is revealed:

> Six Cranes where Baltic vessels come
> With coal to break the strike.
> *'Does Mr Scargill think we think*
> *The revolution starts like this?'* (O'Brien 1987, 23)

Joseph Brooker suggests that the italicised lines are the words of, 'we may guess, a Baltic seaman', who is sardonically posing the question with a tone of 'mocking brutality [...] especially as the poem appeared after the strike's failure' (2010, 89). Although one reading is of a 'Baltic seaman' asking the question to Scargill, it appears to be a much broader 'we' than Brooker affirms. Here, 'we' could be seen as speaking for the NUM members for whom the strikes proved to be a false dawn, the British public at large, who by the end of the strike had generally turned on Scargill, or Thatcher's government. If 'we' is the NUM members and trade unionists more broadly, the question ceases to be mocking and becomes one of disillusionment and discontent.

Between the end of the miners' strike of 1984–5 and the publication of the poem in 1987, 39 collieries had closed down in the UK at a cost of around 39,000 jobs, many of which would have been the jobs of striking miners (Department for Business, Energy & Industrial Strategy 2016). Within this climate of job losses, the question '*Does Mr Scargill think we think / The revolution starts like this?*', if posed by former miners, is one of a loss of faith in Scargill. The implication being that although Scargill continues to preach 'revolution', those who had followed him no longer

---

[4] The report was produced by Conservative MP Nicholas Ridley and outlined the ways in which a Conservative government would be able to defeat another union uprising through the denationalisation of British industry and services.

believe in the project. The 'Mr' establishes a distance and level of formality between the 'we' asking the question and Scargill. The title ('Mr') is not necessarily mocking, however, but perhaps more a form of deference. Although the questioning 'we' may not be following Scargill any longer, there is still a level of respect intimated for this staunchest of trade union champions. What Scargill had achieved is not completely forgotten.

If the question is read as being posed by the state and/or Conservative government—particularly by Margaret Thatcher, who would herself often be referred to as *Mrs* Thatcher—the use of 'Mr' becomes nothing but mockery. Here the use of 'Mr' becomes a title through which to ridicule Scargill, by the act of paying false deference to him. The title elevates Scargill to a position outside and away from his union members (and to an extent the working class he 'represents') and is employed to facilitate his discreditation. The line becomes one where Scargill is shown to be lacking the intellect required to be taken seriously and, as such, insignificant. Not only is Scargill's thinking flawed, but his questionable thinking about others shows him to be disorientated, politically, socially and intellectually. The rhetorical question makes Scargill's reply irrelevant. The poem does not allow him the space to respond. In this sense, the 'we' is both the government's reply and the government speaking on behalf of, and to, a broader public, questioning the intelligence of those who would wish to follow Scargill. The repetition of 'think' in the penultimate line separates the thinking of Scargill, the singular, from the thinking of the 'we', the masses, or 'we' the government. In the poem, after the strike of 1984–5, Scargill no longer represents a mass, at least that is what we are being told. Scargill is only representing himself.

If we take the final two lines—'*Does Mr Scargill think we think / The revolution starts like this*' (O'Brien 1987, 23)—to be spoken by the state, they also become the response to the claim that 'Baltic vessels' are coming to 'break the strike'. The state's response is to ignore these claims and shift the focus onto Scargill's failings. It is only the state that can register and 'unregister'. While the state registers a final response, the poem ends before Scargill has a chance to respond. He is not given the space to speak. The title reasserts itself and it is Scargill's response that is 'unregistered'. His response is not officially recognised, it is not included in the strike narrative. The narrative is completely constructed by the state. The speaker mimics the form of a conversation, while delivering both question and answer. The state registers its response in the form of a question that never requires an answer. The only voices we have left are from those with the platform to tell the public what they should think. The oppositional has been scored from the poem. The labour narrative is solely controlled by the 'dominant' cultural elements.

I.IV Steve Ely's 'Arthur Scargill', 'One of Us', 'Ballad of the Scabs', 'Scum of the Earth' and 'Nithing'

In the poems of Steve Ely, there are a (considerably) greater number of references to Arthur Scargill (and Margaret Thatcher) than in the other poets' work here. Ely gives consideration to the ways alternative voices can challenge dominant narratives, but also to the ways these voices can be silenced. In his debut collection, *Oswald's Book of Hours* (2013), Ely includes the poem 'Arthur Scargill' in a section of the book titled 'Memorial of the Saints'. The back cover of *Oswald's* describes the volume as being 'written in the voices of an unlikely band of northern subversives, including NUM leader Arthur Scargill, hermit Richard Rolle, brigand John Nevison, Catholic rebel Robert Aske'. Unlike the other members of the 'unlikely band' and the figures that make up the 13 'saints', Arthur Scargill is still alive.[5] Scargill has been memorialised by Ely before he has passed away.

Memorials are as much about the act of commemoration as they are the person or thing being remembered or commemorated. As Owen Dwyer and Derek Alderman contend in their work on public memorials, 'memorials are places for social actors and groups to debate and negotiate the right to decide what is commemorated and what version of the past will be made visible to the public' (2008, 171). What becomes memorialised is that which has been chosen to be worthy of memorialisation, the legacy or narrative that is deemed correct or acceptable.

Although the poem is titled 'Arthur Scargill', the character of Scargill never appears; he is simply spoken about as 'you'. What Ely does instead is open the poem by foregrounding the plight of workers, highlighting their narratives and legacies:

> The lowest of the low and low-paid,
> the primary men; farmhands, quarrymen, *colliers*'
> Crude men, of appetite and violence, mumblers,
> white-knucklers, averters of eyes. (2013, 71)

---

[5] The other saints are: Wayne Johnson—who, according to Ely, is 'a fictionalised portrayal of Billy Whitehurst, a South Yorkshire born footballer (Hull City, Newcastle United, Sheffield United and Oxford United), whose on-field physicality and penchant for off-field mayhem gained him the reputation as "England's hardest footballer" during the 1980s and 90s' (2016, 5); Dismas the Good Thief—one of the two thieves being crucified along with Jesus Christ; John Ball (1338–81)—a priest who was a part of the Peasants' Revolt of 1381; John Nevison (1639–84)—a famous highwayman; Joseph the Dreamer—a character from Genesis who could predict the future; Michael the Archangel; Mary Magdalene; Paul, the apostle; Richard Rolle (1290–1349)—hermit and mystic; Robert Aske (1500–37)—leader of a rebellion who was executed by Henry VIII; Robenhode—Robin Hood; Oswald—King of Northumbria.

Ely situates Scargill, and as a corollary his actions during the miners' strikes of the 1970s and 1980s, as a result of the horrendous conditions faced by many, particularly miners—'Crushed torsos under splintered / chocks, amputation on the maingate rip, / blood-streaked phlegm hocked-up' (2013, 71). These 'conditions', be they chronic illness or accident, are all largely avoidable and exist only as a result of the miners' working conditions. There is a tension here between the work of mining essentially killing the workers, yet also being the facilitation for a 'better', albeit largely consumerist, lifestyle. The poem suggests that the worst thing about being exploited in a capitalist system is not simply the physical and mental oppression of said system, but not being able to take part in the consumer benefits which that system creates.

We have no mention of Scargill's strike action or his relationship to the NUM, and it is not until the twelfth line of the sonnet that he is referenced: 'You brought them health and Palma de Mallorca, / Cortinas on the drive and kids in college, / reading Marx and Mao and *The Wealth of Nations*' (Ely 2013, 71). Here, the idea of the poem as 'memorial' can be witnessed. The memorial is being used to commemorate a different, non-strike, aspect of Scargill's legacy. Ely separates Scargill from the legacy of strike action and politicking which so often obscures any further discussion of Scargill's influence.

The final line shifts and sets Scargill as a product of Karl Marx, Mao Zedong and Adam Smith. By leaving these three figures as the final reference points of the sonnet—'Marx and Mao and *The Wealth of Nations*' (Ely 2013, 71)—and omitting Scargill's name from the poem proper, Ely makes Scargill as 'man' less important than the ideologies that drove his actions. Nevertheless, this poem is a 'memorial' to the 'saint' Arthur Scargill, and that memorial is being delivered to Arthur Scargill, the addressed 'you'. There is a need to memorialise Scargill. The implication is that his ideas and political power have passed away, but they still need to be recognised. By ending with the names and works of three revolutionary writers in a poem about the hardships of labour, Ely is attempting to return their ideas to the labouring classes, using Arthur Scargill as a model by which to do so. Socialist learning, against Benjamin Kunkel's comment that socialist learning has become 'a hobby of rich people's children' (2014, 64), is returned to those who drive 'Cortinas' and have come to be excluded from the academic spaces in which people read 'Marx and Mao and *The Wealth of Nations*'. Yet, through all of this, it is still Scargill's name at the top of the page. Scargill is the figure that 'permits' the discussion of these labour narratives. Although the political concerns of the poem seem to exceed Scargill, he is the gateway through which the working classes can access their labour histories.

*

In Ely's follow-up collection, *Englaland*, Arthur Scargill is directly referenced in five of the poems: 'Ballad of the Scabs', 'The Ballad of Dave Hart', 'One of Us', 'Nithing' and the playlet 'Scum of the Earth'. Through references to Scargill in these works, Ely uses the manipulation of naming to demonstrate the ways 'effective dominant cultures' seek to incorporate or discredit alternative labour narratives, and how these narratives attempt to resist incorporation.

The title of the poem, 'One of Us', is a reference to Margaret Thatcher's stock 'is he one of us?' question, 'asked of impartial civil servants and even would-be bishops' (White 2013, n.pag.). Scargill is not one of Thatcher's 'us', but he is part of the working classes. In 'One of Us', we have Ely's only mention of Arthur Scargill as the mythical 'King Arthur'. Yet there is something of a tension between Scargill as 'king' and the claiming of Scargill as 'us':

> [...] Cecil, with his boyish smile, brylcreemed hair,
> and a side-parting to set your watch to.
> A Carnforth railman's lad, hauled himself up
> by his eh-bah-gum braces, grammar school,
> Cambridge, millionaire, Tory MP.
> Then Chairman of the Party v Arthur Scargill
> on Question Time. King Arthur, the Cossack-quiffed
> syndicalist from nah-then-lad Worsborough [*sic*] Dale,
> President of the NUM via White Cross
> Secondary Modern, Woolley Pit and the diehard
> red-raggers of Yorkshire, the real Yorkshire. (Ely 2015, 120)

The 'Cecil' referenced is Cecil Parkinson, who held the position of Chairman of the Conservative Party between 1981 and 1983.[6] He was one of Thatcher's 'us'. Although Arthur Scargill and Cecil Parkinson both frequently appeared on *Question Time*, they were never to appear on the same occasion. This staging of Scargill and Parkinson is, in effect, a fabrication by Ely. These two figures are brought into the poem where they are then used as counterpoints to one another. The line 'Then Chairman of the Party v Arthur Scargill' echoes Harrison's 'vs'—'man v. wife, / Communist v. Fascist, Left v. Right / class v. class as bitter as before' (2008, 11)—and, accordingly, places the poem as part of a longer poetic 'narrative' of strike literature.

---

[6] Cecil Parkinson had served as the first Secretary of State for Trade and Industry in Thatcher's government in 1983. He was replaced less than six months after taking the position by Norman Tebbit, having resigned his post in October 1983 after details of an affair he'd been having with his secretary, and her subsequent pregnancy, were revealed (Grice 2016, n.pag.).

Ely's driving interest seems to lie within the concept of institutional systems and the relationship between those systems and a personal politics. Cecil Parkinson appears on *Question Time* as 'Chairman of the Party', a representative of a system of politics he has helped shape and disseminate. He was elected as a Tory MP, but Chairman of the Party is a position handed to him. Conversely, Scargill appears as 'Arthur Scargill', his allegiance to the NUM portrayed as secondary to his politics. Scargill is one man against the 'Party'. Arthur Scargill is included in the poem due to his legacy, whereas Cecil Parkinson, referred to initially in the poem as 'Cecil'—a tactic which serves to confer a false tone of familiarity based on their shared working-class roots—requires justification for his inclusion, which he receives when Ely asserts that he was '*then* Chairman of the Party'. Cecil Parkinson's justification comes from a position he held over thirty years ago.

Parkinson's potted biography traces a relatively chronological and conservatively 'meritocratic' path from his own working-class beginnings— 'railman's lad'—through his education, to his position in the Conservative Party—'grammar school, / Cambridge, millionaire, Tory MP' (Ely 2015, 120). Scargill's history starts with him on *Question Time*, before shifting to 'King Arthur', through to his political views ('syndicalist'), his birthplace and his position within the National Union of Mineworkers, before returning to his education and work life—'via White Cross / Secondary Modern, Woolley Pit and the diehard / red-raggers of Yorkshire' (Ely 2015, 120). Cecil Parkinson's rise to the position of 'Chairman of the Party' comes through decisions which distance him from his working-class roots. 'Cecil' is pushed into the background and what remains is the system into which he is drawn. Ely's Scargill is from 'Worsborough Dale', while *also* being 'President of the NUM'. If Parkinson is presented as leaving behind 'Carnforth' and his 'eh-bah-gum' accent for 'learned RP' and the Tory party (Ely 2015, 120), Scargill's 'Worsborough Dale' is intrinsically tied up in his position as 'King Arthur' and 'President of the NUM'. Scargill's position and valorisation come via his work experiences and his connection to his working-class roots. For Ely, Scargill speaks in 'our flat South Riding vowels', with 'consonants blunt as cobbles, arguments sharp as a diamond bit' (2015, 120). Parkinson's language is a 'learned' one. It is a language from which his background has been erased. Scargill's language is one that comes imbued with experiences that allow his legacy to speak to broader labour narratives.

Unlike the valorisation of Scargill, Thatcher is dismissed in the first line of the poem—'The good looking, charming man Margaret / always had a soft spot for' (Ely 2015, 120). Ely's characterisation of Thatcher as 'Margaret', through the use of the overly familiar first name and as someone who had a 'soft spot' for Parkinson because he was 'good looking', refuses to engage with Thatcher as politician and removes her agency. For a poem that is ostensibly not about Margaret Thatcher (she never appeared on *Question Time*), to open with a reference to her in relation to a 'charming man' speaks to a more general neglect of women within these strike poems. Even the first woman Prime Minister is still powerless before the 'boyish smile' of Cecil Parkinson, a minister junior to her. Reducing Thatcher, however toxic her actions and legacy, to the role of charmed woman does not challenge her or her legacy.

The confrontation between Parkinson and Scargill establishes a situation where the social power and legacy of each is challenged and perpetuated. The dominant social power within the poem is that of the working classes, particularly those of 'the real Yorkshire' (Ely 2015, 120). Williams claims that 'it is a fact about the modes of domination, that they select from and consequently exclude the full range of human practice' (1977, 125). Yet Ely situates social power with the 'oppositional' groups, and registers 'meanings and values as they are actively lived and felt, and the relations between these and formal or systematic beliefs' (Williams 1977, 132). Scargill's appearance on *Question Time* is used as a platform for the oppositional. Scargill's speech inspires the narrator to join the 'CND, Anti-Nazi League / and the Socialist Workers Party', and has such an impact that the poem ends with a pledge of everlasting patronage, 'Arthur Scargill / We'll support you evermore' (Ely 2015, 120–1).

Although laudatory, there is still a tension with the ostensibly singular voice of the poem speaking for, but not necessarily as, the 'we'. The chant for Scargill in these final lines increases this tension. A chant allows individual voices to disappear, while requiring a certain consensus to continue. So, by the end of the poem, who is this 'we'? In an inverse of Mort's 'Scab' and Harrison's 'V.', where the final lines of the poem position the reader as 'you', Ely's 'we' claims the reader. The 'we' in the poem becomes co-opted into Ely's political history and implicated in Scargill's fall from prominence. He is now in need of support, yet this support is not forthcoming.[7] 'We'll support you evermore' is rhetoric. The poem's line break separates Scargill from the pledge of support. Ely's return to the use of Scargill's full name in the closing of the poem points towards a public consciousness in which the name 'Arthur' is no longer enough. It becomes necessary for 'Arthur Scargill' to be spelled out in full, even when talking to those that support

---

[7] This support may well also be in reference to the legal battles that Scargill had been fighting with the NUM pertaining to a flat that was being paid for by the union: 'We now know, for example, that until late 2012, the NUM paid £34,000 a year in rent for his council flat in the Barbican in London—and that in 1993, he tried to use the Right to Buy scheme pioneered by Thatcher to buy it. Scargill says that if he had succeeded, the property would eventually have been returned to the union; the NUM's leadership insists there is no evidence to back up this claim' (Harris 2014, n.pag.; 'Arthur Scargill Loses London Flat Case' 2012, n.pag.).

him. If there are any supporters left, they are supporting a legacy that is fading.

*

This usage of 'Arthur Scargill' suggesting a lack of public awareness does not hold true, however, through Ely's other poems in *Englaland*. In 'Ballad of the Scabs', there is a clear political distance between 'Arthur Scargill' and 'Scargill'. It is 'Arthur Scargill' who 'saw it true' and said that the Conservatives would 'destroy our jobs and communities / within a single year' (Ely 2015, 137), yet it is 'Scargill' who is on the receiving end of a lawsuit:

> Sir Hector Laing stumped up some cash
> Lord Hanson stumped up more
> they served a writ on Scargill
> on the Labour Conference floor.
>
> A firm of Tory lawyers
> deployed the state machine
> and outlawed Scargill and the NUM
> to the silence of the TUC. (Ely 2015, 139)[8]

Scargill is presented without a title, in contrast to the honorifics of Sir Hector Laing and Lord Hanson. It is 'Arthur Scargill' who is an icon of political foresight and 'Scargill' who is a member of the trade union movement. Similarly, in 'The Ballad of Dave Hart', Hart is spoken of as 'the man who broke the NUM / and Arthur Scargill's power' (Ely 2015, 122).[9] There is a prestige in breaking 'Arthur Scargill's power' which is not there with 'Scargill'. In 'Ballad of the Scabs', Hector Laing and James Hanson, both of whom were Conservative Party supporters and financial backers—

---

[8] Laing and Hanson were instrumental in helping to finance what would become the Union of Democratic Mineworkers, a group made up of 'dissident' miners (Milne 2014, 325).

[9] Hart was one of the main organisers and financial backers of the back-to-work movement during the 1984–5 strike, and was responsible for touring 'mining areas in a Mercedes driven by his chauffeur' and 'organizing a network of disaffected and strikebreaking miners' (Milne 2014, 324). Hart had also planned and was granted planning permission to build a '23ft gold-tipped Egyptian-style' pyramid-shaped mausoleum out of stone, glass and gold on the grounds of his home, Chadacre Hall (Watson-Smyth 2000, n.pag.). Unfortunately, according to a local newspaper article from when the house was sold in 2010, the pyramid was never completed (Goss 2010, n.pag.).

Laing also acting as the party treasurer in the late 1980s—are referred to by their official honorifics, 'Sir' and 'Lord', respectively. By reducing Arthur Scargill's full name to only 'Scargill', and avoiding the 'King' designation he had employed in 'One of Us', Ely sets up a clear demarcation between those indebted to the state, who are part of a dominant cultural order, and those who are controlled by it. For Laing and Hanson, Scargill is never and could never be 'King'.

*

In the playlet 'Scum of the Earth', Ely has two members of the nobility, 'Arthur Wellesley, Field Marshal His Grace the First Duke of Wellington' and 'Peter Benjamin, The Right Honourable Lord Mandelson of Foy in the County of Hereford, and Hartlepool in the County of Durham' competing for the affections of a 'Chorus of the Swinish Multitude' before a 'momentous battle in a second English Civil War' (Ely 2015, 43).[10] The specificity of their titles, albeit correctly ascribed when referring to Wellesley and Mandelson— Wellesley and Mandelson is how they are then referred to in the rest of the work—against the homogenised (and derogatory) 'swinish multitude', continues Ely's interrogation in *Englaland* of authority and rhetoric through the manipulation of naming. Mandelson rallies his troops of 'consumers and customers, stakeholders in the United Kingdom of Great Britain and Northern Ireland PLC' with cries of capitalism and free marketeering, in line with New Labour's own political vision (Ely 2015, 44), while Wellesley promises 'England for the English' and a future filled with 'freebooting, fighting and the fancy' (Ely 2015, 50, 54). The play finally comes to a close with the 'swines' recognising their common identity and interests and turning on those 'who keep us irate / on jingo and hate' (Ely 2015, 57, 59).

'Scargill' is on two occasions invoked by the character Mandelson as a symbol of a backwards-looking and more barbarous Britain. The first instance of Scargill in the poem has Mandelson proclaiming that '*Maggie. Minden. Maldon.* Their past is past, / like sturgeon, Scargill and jobs-for-life: / their future belongs to us' (Ely 2015, 47).[11] Margaret

[10] In the 2001 UK General Election, Peter Mandelson (Labour) and Arthur Scargill (SLP) both contested the electoral seat for Hartlepool. Mandelson won with 59.1 per cent of the vote (22,506 of 38,051 total votes cast), Scargill came fourth with only 2.4 per cent (912 votes) ('Vote 2001: Results and Constituencies: Hartlepool' 2001, n.pag.).

[11] The slogan 'the future belongs to us' is one that has traditionally been employed by fascists. The earliest usage I have found is from an interview given by Kaiser Wilhelm II in 1908 to *Century Magazine* (Hale 2014, n.pag.). The slogan has also been used by Donald Trump at a Conservative Political Action Group conference (Smith & Siddiqui 2017, n.pag.).

Thatcher is placed alongside the Battle of Minden, fought in 1759, and the Battle of Maldon in 991. Interestingly, the poems 'recounting' these battles, Rudyard Kipling's 'The Men that Fought at Minden' and the Old English poem 'The Battle of Maldon', are many people's introduction to the battles themselves. In the case of the Battle of Maldon, 'the poem is our only detailed source', so that much of our historical knowledge of the battle originates from the poem itself (Dean 1992, 100). Poems are not a history, but they can be part of a narrative. However, as Paul Dean goes on to claim, 'even if the poem could be shown to be of the late tenth century it would still be apparent that the society and social codes it reflects are fabricated' and that the poem may have no historical 'status in relation to the events it describe' (1992, 100). It is not simply that these social codes are 'fabricated', but that the poems reveal something about how (and why) these codes came to be established.[12]

Ely's reference to these two battles in 'Scum' raises questions about how we create histories and suggests that art, in this instance poetry, can play a role in, and is complicit with, informing these narratives. If we return to Dean's quotations, we can see that Ely is highlighting the 'fabricated' nature of social codes and the folly of attempting to read concretising narratives from poems. As well as the simply alliterative quality, by placing '*Maggie*' alongside '*Minden*' and '*Maldon*', not only is Thatcher aligned with notions of war and conquest, but of having a history that is itself informed as much by cultural products and second-hand narratives, as it is by her actions. '*Maggie. Minden. Maldon*' is an obvious bastardisation of the '*Maggie. Maggie. Maggie. Out. Out. Out*' chant. Altering the words of the chant serves to question the nature of such rhetoric, but also the ease with which groups from outside traditionally socially dominant groups can have their language co-opted and appropriated by groups and individuals that do not represent them.

However, it is Wellesley who first utters the name 'Maggie' to his troops with the rhetorical question, 'Is this the England of Maggie and Mafeking, / Waterloo and Winston, Dunkirk and Drake?' (Ely 2015, 47). Wellesley's utterance is one to inspire his troops and has at its heart an aspiration to return to the 'social codes' that these historical figures and events, and their associations with war and nationalism, are envisioned as representing. While Mandelson's '*Maggie*' is a mocking response to Wellesley, both speeches show a political figurehead telling the populace,

---

[12] Kipling's poem 'The Men that Fought at Minden' comes from the voice of an experienced army recruit who is advising a group of new trainees on the decorums of the British Army, while recounting, and forgetting, details of those who fought at the Battle of Minden. Our introduction to the battle is unreliable. Yet this 'history' is supported by the speaker's supposed authority as an experienced military recruit.

regardless of which side they are on, which parts of their cultural history *should* hold meaning for them. Whether this cultural history requires a reapproximation (Wellesley) or a negation (Mandelson) of cultural histories is less significant than the essential struggle over the modes by which dominant and, as a consequence, oppositional elements of culture can be controlled. Ely is critiquing both Wellesley and Mandelson in 'Scum'. He presents apparently contrasting modes of rhetoric to show them both to be wanting. This rhetoric proves so inadequate that at one point 'a swine' is forced to ask, perplexed, what 'the fuck's he on about?' (Ely 2015, 49). The 'multitude' do not recognise the retelling of their own histories.

As Mandelson refers to Scargill, even while telling us his 'past is past', we are left with questions concerning what it means to construct labour histories, and the ways in which inclusion or exclusion from dominant labour narratives can be manipulated to serve a particular political end. If 'their past is past', for the likes of 'sturgeon, Scargill and jobs-for-life', why need we be reminded of it? (Ely 2015, 47). Reiterating claims for something's supposed demise suggests a fear that the thing professed to be obsolete may not be so. Conversely, it is an attempt to renew an anxiety about returning to a version of the past deemed to be contemptible by some. In 'Scum', Mandelson's second invocation of Scargill appears to lean towards the latter reading:

> And there we have it. The England of Scargill
> and Ian Stuart Donaldson via F-Troop
> and Harry the Dog. Grisly as Griffin,
> gruesome as Galloway—dead as Dave Nellist. (Ely 2015, 52)

Scargill's name is used as the figurehead for a list that includes: the white supremacist 'Ian Stuart Donaldson', lead singer of Screwdriver, a white-power band; England's most notorious football hooligan firm and one of their 'stars', 'F-troop / and Harry the Dog'; the former leader of the far-right British National Party, Nick Griffin; leader of the now dissolved far-left Respect party and media personality George Galloway; and a (not deceased) former Labour MP who was the Chair of the Trade Union and Socialist Coalition, Dave Nellist. It is clear that Mandelson is proposing a form of moderate, centrist politics, one that excludes the more 'radical' factions of the political spectrum. However, the fact that Mandelson conjures these names into a single space seeds the idea that these people should be considered together and, perhaps, share some commonalities. It shows how our narratives can come to be populated by figures and ideas that are not part of them. Ely is questioning a form of (centrist) populist rhetoric that would seek to flatten political difference and homogenise narratives.

Ely's reference of Scargill works not only as a critique, but as a comment on the political and cultural impact Scargill has had. It is the 'England of Scargill' foremost, the other 'characters' are secondary. Mandelson is unintentionally reinvoking Scargill's 'legacy' while trying to silence the legacy he believes Scargill has left. This legacy is both Scargill's own and that of the trade union movement more broadly. The others are referred to by their full names or are given alliterative nicknames to remind the audience, both the 'swinish multitude' and the reader, of who they are and why they matter. And while Nick Griffin and George Galloway suffer a bastardisation from Mandelson, Scargill is there through the cultural weight of his surname. We see the beginnings of the naming tropes Ely employs in 'Ballad of the Scabs', where it is the figure of 'Scargill' that is attacked by the state. Mandelson's speech serves to demonstrate the levels of (attempted) control perpetrated by the state in regard to political 'dissention'. There is a fear that comes from Scargill's legacy and influence. By discrediting Scargill and his name, there is an attempt to control the labour narratives that are so tied up with his legacy.

At the end of his speech, Mandelson tells his audience that our 'nation can be whatever we want it to be' (Ely 2015, 53). If something can be 'whatever we want', it implies a lack of restriction, yet also a lack of direction in the outcome. Mandelson telling his audience that our 'nation' can be anything comes after a detailed list of what we should be celebrating, a form of globalised capitalism: 'the City and our blue-chip exports— / global warming, Coldplay, Wallace & Gromit' (Ely 2015, 53). If a nation can be 'whatever we want it to be', it means that our histories can also be whatever we want them to be. Wellesley and Mandelson construct their histories along different lines, yet use them in homologous ways to garner support from the poem's populace. Placing Wellesley and Mandelson together directs our attention to the ways that political narratives succumb to manipulation, and how the selective practices that go into constructing these narratives work to justify a political present.

*

In Ely's 'Nithing', what we have is a symbol of the end of Anglo-Saxon rule, the institution of French as the language of England and a concerted oppression of the northern peoples of England. The poem opens by welcoming us to 'the Theatre of Hate':

> *Harold*, the English King;
> *William*, Duke of Normandy;
> *Arthur*, President of the NUM;
> *Ian*, Chairman of the NCB, and;
> *Margaret*, Prime Minister of the United Kingdom of
> Great Britain and Northern Ireland. (Ely 2015, 124)

The inclusion of William the Conqueror and Harold Godwinson ties into the overarching concerns of the section of *Englaland*, 'The Harrowing of the North', from which 'Nithing' is taken. Ely's concerns with the historical adoption and enforcement of language, plus opposition to such measures, are played out through the figures of Margaret Thatcher and Arthur Scargill. According to Ely's explanatory notes on the poem in *Digging the Seam: Popular Cultures of the 1984/5 Miners' Strike*, 'Nithing' is an 'Old English word denoting a man so contemptible, that any honourable man had an obligation to slay him on sight' (Ely 2012, 130). What follows is a failed assassination attempt on Margaret Thatcher and three on Scargill.[13]

After our introduction to the 'Theatre of Hate', Thatcher's next appearance in the poem comes in the form of a chant, interspersed with somewhat graphic body horror:

> *Maggie Maggie Maggie*
> The nithing must be scolded
> To force it to reveal
>
> *Ut Ut Ut*
> it seems to be a woman
> and yet
> An eelpout coils
> in the slimy gusset
> *Every woman's got one*
> birther of werewolves
> catfish and zander
> *Maggie is one*
> hermaphrodite self-fucker
> The lubricated head
> of the butterfish
> Wriggling through the sphincter
> *Maggie Maggie Maggie*
>
> *Ut Ut Ut.* (Ely 2015, 124)

---

[13] The attempt on Thatcher's life was made in the Brighton hotel bombing on 12 October 1984 during the Conservative Party Conference. Although there are no 'official' reports relating to the attempts to assassinate Scargill—Ely's notes say that Scargill chose not to report them 'in order to maintain the morale of the strikers' (2012, 130)—Scargill himself said, in a 2005 interview for the Irish Republican paper *An Phoblacht*, that there were five assassination attempts on him during the strike and shortly after, which the media did not report (Scargill 2005, n.pag.).

In a review of Hugo Young's biography of Thatcher, *The Iron Lady* (1989), Martin Amis states that 'the only interesting thing about Mrs Thatcher is that she isn't a man' and that 'onlookers seems to share the same anxiety: that one day Mrs T. will start heading for the wrong toilet' (2002, 19). Amis's misogynistic statement ties into some of the apparent anxieties emanating from Ely's narrator, namely that Thatcher may be a woman, but she is not enough of one. In the same way that Ely's 'Inglan is a Bitch' doesn't really interrogate the gender issues inherent in its title, with the poem working as a critique of Great Britain more broadly, the determined focus on the 'villainous' Thatcher in 'Nithing' is an issue. While the portrait painted in the poem is exaggerated and grotesque, it is still one of the few extended engagements we have with Thatcher, or any woman, across these strike poems. As raised in relation to 'One of Us', however, the fact Ely's mode of 'challenge' to Thatcher is through her being a woman does present this as being in some way instructive as to our understanding of her.

The reference to a 'hermaphrodite' is telling. Hermaphroditism in literature is, Sarah Carter argues, 'paradoxically a symbol of union and conflict, of perfection and monstrosity, of proto-feminism and homoeroticism' (2010, 107). In line with Carter, with the focus on Thatcher's body and sexual reproduction, there is a level not only of fear but also of fascination. With Thatcher being 'accused' of adopting the traits of traditional masculinity—traits undoubtedly required to become the first female Prime Minister in British history—there is an attempt to use these to undermine her. Thatcher is not referred to as 'she', but as an 'it'. As an 'it', Thatcher 'appears to be a woman'. The fear stems not from being a 'woman', but from Thatcher looking like a woman is 'supposed' to and yet not behaving as one is 'expected'. There is a difficulty of reconciling the image of Thatcher with her actions.

Considering these issues of misinformation and naming alongside the chant that runs through the quoted section of the poem, Ely is illuminating a wider structure of misinformation that exists in labour and political narratives. Not only does the chant refer to Thatcher by the overly informal 'Maggie', which serves as an attempt to 'dethrone' her from her position as PM, but it imagines a community of people speaking through a single voice. As the 'chant' bookends the above-quoted section of the poem, what we read is the chant, ostensibly calling on Margaret Thatcher to leave office, holding within its rhetoric a more troubling multitude of submerged and repressed fears surrounding misinformation and gender. The chant allows voices to hide behind and within this supposedly singular call. It drowns out some voices and allows others to flourish with some impunity. As fragments of the chant become interspersed with the graphic animal imagery, the chant becomes that which both perpetuates the narrative and tries to refocus it. Each cry of the chant can be read as justifying that which has gone before it, each grotesque representation being met with an affirmation by the chant or as a spur to continue. Simultaneously, the chant attempts to 'correct' the narrative, from the polemic of Thatcher as 'creature' and back to that of her as a political figure.

It is as a political figure that Thatcher has to be challenged. By configuring her as 'monster', even metaphorically, we remove Thatcher's culpability and construct her solely as a product of her nature, not of her actions. Ely is demonstrating the way in which narratives can be hijacked and repurposed so that what these narratives mean is constantly being negotiated. By the end of the excerpt, it is impossible to claim that *'Maggie Maggie Maggie / Ut Ut Ut'* solely means what it did at the beginning. By the time we arrive at the final two lines, our reading of the chant has picked up and become coloured by that which it has been exposed to. Although a chant is predicated on a group shouting or singing in unison, it would be amiss to treat any group as having a fully homogeneous politics, regardless of the outward expression of uniformity. This type of rhetoric can be used to obscure desires and drives, while personal narratives rarely express or account for the narratives of others. Similarly, (our) narratives become part of other narratives, over which we have no control. These narratives, by combining and growing larger and more vociferous, become *the* narrative, a narrative that is both an approximation of all the narrative voices and one in which the individual cannot be heard.

*

In these poems, the shift in naming points to the way individuals become subsumed by larger political agendas. The legacies of Scargill and Thatcher are used as a way to advance particular labour narratives and to discredit others. These narratives are managed through 'reinterpretation, dilution, projection' and 'discriminating inclusion and exclusion' (Williams 1977, 123). The way the names of Scargill and Thatcher come to be manipulated and presented expose our labour narratives as a construction. These constructions seek to silence alternative voices and control the way labour narratives are received and understood. In controlling strike narratives, there is also an attempt by those in power who fear the power of collective action to control the responses to labour histories and labour presents.

CHAPTER FOUR

Strikes and Place

> There is a universally shared ache to return to the place we left behind or to found a new home in which our hopes for the future can nest and grow [...] Home need not always correspond to a single dwelling or place. We can choose its form and location but not its meaning.
> Shoshana Zuboff, *The Age of Surveillance Capitalism* (2019)

How we consider our places, and our relationship to those places, are a product of the ways in which the places (and their narratives) we inhabit have been manipulated. As Doreen Massey argues in her article 'Places and their Pasts', 'if the past transforms the present, helps thereby to make it, so too does the present make the past' (1995, 187). Our ideas about our pasts shape how we think about our present relationship with a place but, simultaneously, our thinking about our present is directly responsible for the stories that are told regarding a place's history. Massey also writes that histories of our past 'are constructed so as to confirm the views and convictions of the present' (1995, 186). Histories are told from the present. To tell the stories and histories of a place is to select the stories that confirm our current relationship with a place as being correct or valid (if this relationship is 'functional'), or to tell stories that highlight and question a present and 'dysfunctional' relationship with a place.

This chapter focuses on the works of Bentley, Mort and Ely and their conceptions of place, particularly in regard to the north-east of England, and the appropriation of strike narratives of the 1984–5 miners' strike. The ways in which stories are told about strike histories (and the legacy they have) are a patchwork of conflicting voices and acts of cultural appropriation. Through this appropriation, these narratives come to exclude those people they are supposed to represent.

*

Strikes and Place

Most pit villages were constructed around the time of the Industrial Revolution to house miners employed in the newly established mines of England and Wales. With the closure of all deep pits in the United Kingdom, the 'purpose' of these villages ceased to exist. Robert Chesshyre, in an article for the *Independent* about the Easington Colliery and the pit village that surrounds it, points out that 'pit villages only existed because they sat on coal' and that by removing the pit 'you remove the heart of the community' (Chesshyre 2013). If we were to frame Chesshyre's assertion in slightly more critical terms, by closing the pit an individual's relationship with, and how they define themselves in relation to, a place is forced into a situation in which the nature of their relationship must be re-examined. The terms on which the relationship was built no longer exist, and such a relationship is unable to function productively. How we see ourselves and the narratives that we tell regarding a place become vulnerable to appropriation by those who seek to exploit said place and its narratives.

Massey asserts that 'the identity of places is very much bound up with the histories which are told of them, how these histories are told, and which history turns out to be dominant' (1995, 187). As Massey's statement suggests, our histories are pluralised, they are multi-vocal. Yet they are caught up in battles for dominance. The poems in this chapter navigate the particular legacies of strikes in the north-east to show how the people these legacies are supposed to represent have been alienated from them. If, has been argued, the 1984–5 miners' strike was formally national, but characteristically regional (Samuel 1986, 20), what we encounter when talking about place in regard to the strike is a tension between the desire to create grand narratives and establish uniform legacies and the aim, simultaneously, of doing justice to a place's 'particular history and character' (Gibbon & Steyne 1986, 8).

I. Paul Bentley's 'The Two Magicians'

In 'The Two Magicians' Bentley attempts to mediate between collective and singular voices to expose how geographical legacies come to be constructed and appropriated. A curious element of the poem are the 'Solo' and 'Chorus' sections that Bentley employs, almost as a poetic footnote to the main text. To give an example of what I am referring to, in the 'King Arthur' section quoted in the previous chapter, Bentley's text and Chorus appear as follows:

> Johnny Marr's guitar screaming, echoing—
> Mum's *Turn that down I can't hear myself think!*
> Two boys on top of the pile, picking coal.
>   Me thoughts I heard one calling: Child.

Chorus:

There was a women's picket arranged for Cresswell ... The police were mesmerised at first. We got up to the pit gates, then all these vans came flying up. They tried to keep us in one spot, so we started walking up and down. One of the inspectors was getting a bit uppity, 'You stay there, you say nothing'. But this time we did say something. (2011, 12)

All of the instances of the Chorus in the poem—of which there are six—and the Solo—of which there is only one—are taken verbatim from Gibbon and Steyne's 1986 book *Thurcroft, A Village and the Miners' Strike*. The book's cover says it is 'an oral history by the people of Thurcroft'. What exactly is meant by 'oral history' is outlined in the editors' preface, which provides an account of the process by which the book was assembled and came to be:

We interviewed over fifty people, and finished up with over ninety hours of tape. So that the Thurcrofters could retain control of the project, these tapes were transcribed and passed back to those interviewed for editing. The revised versions were then indexed by topic and issue, and assembled into a coherent story. (Gibbon & Steyne 1986, 7)

What is clear from Gibbon and Steyne's preface is that the book's claim to being oral history comes with something of a caveat: those who were interviewed were able to edit the transcriptions of their interviews. The oral aspect of the reminiscences, once transcribed, becomes a text (or series of texts) which can be 'assembled' and given the appearance of coherence. The oral becomes our entrance to a history, our way of gaining access to the stories that people tell, but that oral history reaches us in an edited form. In *Thurcroft*, the oral is the raw material, used to tell a story that is both 'truthful and positive'. It is also a story which explicitly omits 'purely abusive statements', apart from when they helpfully 'contribute to the depiction of a mood' (Gibbon & Steyne 1986, 7). *Thurcroft* attempts to depict the (positive) mood, of a particular place, during the miners' strike of 1984–5. The issue that arises is that this oral contribution has itself been edited. Setting out to produce a work that is both 'truthful and positive', regarding one of the most economically ruinous events in post-war Britain, is also an attempt to establish a particular type of reading regarding the dispute. With the book published so soon after the strike had ended, there is an attempt on the part of those affected to form their own narrative, before it can be co-opted or dismissed.

In *Thurcroft*, for each quotation we are provided with a name, or more commonly a letter, from which a brief biographical description can be found in the book's index. For the Chorus section from 'The Two Magicians' quoted above, we are told in *Thurcroft* that it is 'G' who contributed the reminiscence. We are told that 'G' is female: 'late 40s Widow. Native and resident of Thurcroft area. Mining family background. (Sister of AA). Pit canteen worker. WAG activist' (Gibbon & Steyne 1986, 271).[1] Bentley does not give us this information for his choruses. The fact that these biographical details are supplied to us in *Thurcroft*, particularly in light of the anonymisation of proper names, is surprising. The implication is that, in a book in which most names are anonymised, we are still encouraged to reflect upon the individuality of the speaker, or at least given sufficient information to be able to ascertain where these utterances came from.[2] This individuality is categorised through their gender, age, marital status, place of residence, family history, employment status and the 'role' played during the 1984–5 strike. However, we do have to seek out this information ourselves, and while readily available at the rear of the book, after each quotation in the main text we are only given the letter. Nevertheless, the text is submitted as 'their story of the strike' (Gibbon & Steyne 1986, 7). It is the collective story of Thurcroft, or the attempt to tell and construct a story of 'a village and the miners' strike'. In the book, we have a range of voices telling us individual stories that are used to construct a grander (singular) tale about a pit village. There is an attempt to synthesise a cohesive strike narrative. Bentley is taking 'their story' for his own, contemporary, narrative. What Bentley's poem does that *Thurcroft* cannot is put these narratives into direct conversation with the legacy that has been established in the wake of the miners' strike.

The editors go so far as to say:

> No claim is made for the typicality of Thurcroft as a 'British pit village'. The activities and experiences of Thurcrofters were shaped in part by the village's particular history and character. To the extent that this is true of all particular villages, there is no 'typical British pit village'. (Gibbon & Steyne 1986, 8)

If there is no typical 'pit village', then there is no typical strike narrative. The strike of 1984–5, 'though national in form, was regional in character' (Samuel 1986, 20). In Nottingham, for example, 'fewer than 2000 men finished the year on strike from a total workforce of nearly 32,000' (Paterson 2014, 11). Yet, even going into the strike, as Bob Fryer notes,

---

[1] 'AA' is another person interviewed for the book. 'WAG' stands for Women's Action Group.

[2] The only names we are given are those of branch officers who are 'describing or reflecting upon their public work as officers, and political activists past and present not employed by the NCB or resident in the village' (Gibbon & Steyne 1986, 7–8).

the great danger of divisions opening up within the NUM was evident from the outset: Nottinghamshire and the rest of the Midland coalfields were likely to be a problem and bitter memories of unsupported struggles in 1983 in South Wales and Scotland necessitated vigorous campaigns to secure widespread support for the strike. (1985, 70)

While the miners were part of a national union, the major drive for many would have been the protection and continuation of their own jobs, at their own pit. Even if this were not the case, each pit's own danger of closure, its productivity at the time and its geographical situation would necessitate the level of support the striking miners might receive from locals and the NUM itself. Each region experienced its own version of the 1984–5 miners' strike.[3]

Returning to 'The Two Magicians', we might ask what has happened now that the quotation by 'G' regarding the 'women's picket arranged for Cresswell' has been separated from the voices which previously surrounded it and now come to be reconfigured as the Chorus? In the instances where Bentley quotes from *Thurcroft* for the Chorus and Solo, the individual attributions have been removed. However, after the first, and only, 'Solo' in the poem—'*Morning, wankers!*' (2011, 8)—Bentley does tell his reader that the 'Solo and Chorus speeches are from *Thurcroft: A Village and the Miners' Strike: An Oral History* by the People of Thurcroft' (2011, 8). We are aware that the quotations come from 'people', plural. By omitting even the brief lettered attribution and biographical information from the source material, these quotations act almost as a disembodied, generalised voice of a place and time. Bentley himself said in email correspondence with me that his

---

[3] Lewis Minkin, in his book on the relationship between the Labour Party and trade unions, writes that 'the NUM was not a united union—much of the large Nottinghamshire Area refused to participate, neither did some other sectors. And it was not a united trade union movement which operated alongside it; some union leaderships [...] were politically alienated and heavily and publicly critical of the lack of a ballot and the picketing tactics involved' (1991, 136). Kim Howells notes the initial reluctance in Wales 'to take the lead once again in confronting a national government', as 'South Wales had led every major coal stoppage since the balmy days of the mid-1970s'. This reluctance to lead was down to a sense that 'they would find themselves isolated in splendid heroism—ready to be picked off one by one after returning to work with their tails between their legs' (1985, 140). Even at its most domestic, Natalie Butts-Thompson and Deborah Price, in the oral history project *How Black Were Our Valleys*, make the passing reference that 'people would put you up in their houses for a week in North Wales and usually about two or three days at a time in the Midlands' (2014, 6). While both are altruistic acts, the difference does speak to an idea of the character of the strike having a decidedly regional edge.

> original idea was to represent directly quoted voices from the mining community as the chorus, and to play these off against the voice of the police, which would form the Solo. The idea was to represent the individual voices of the mining community as a community of voices, and the voice of the police as representing the aggressively individualist ethos of the Tory government—hence the 'Solo'. (2 Mar. 2017)

The 'Solo', as mentioned before, is literally solo in Bentley's poem, it appears only once. Bentley's early intention to have the voice of the 'Solo' reappear throughout the poem, in dialogue with the Chorus, is not carried out in the published text, there being only one police 'voice' in *Thurcroft*. By using the terms 'Chorus' and 'Solo', Bentley does distinguish between the many voices from the mining community and the single voice of the police. While Bentley describes the police as representing 'an aggressively individualist ethos', ironically, this voice could itself be seen as forming part of a collective. The 'police' in the poem is a singular voice, but also the voice of a larger police force and the voice of the state. Even then, the 'voice' is not that of a police officer, but of Pat Fortune, NUM Branch President, recounting what a police officer is supposed to have said to the miners:

> We'd not said a word, but the words that met us on our own pit lane from somebody down south, who if they were on their own in our village would probably shit themselves, was *'Morning, wankers!'* (Gibbon & Steyne 1986, 113)

In this anecdote, it is not so much what the police officer said, but the way Fortune frames it in terms of place that is of most interest. Bentley has removed the questions that Fortune poses regarding place, leaving the poem with the simple declarative, *'Morning, wankers!'* Bentley says that he intended to show the 'individualist ethos' of the Tory government, yet he does it through the shout of a 'policeman', told to us through the reminiscences of a striker, quoted from another text. Bentley does not include what seems to be Fortune's main thrust: it is the fact of the police officer's being from 'down south', and not simply calling the strikers 'wankers' but doing so 'on our own pit lane', that seems to anger him. For Fortune, the issue is as much about place as it is about politics—or it is about the politics of place. The voice from 'down south' heard in their (northern) pit lane is an occupying one. It is there to control the strikers and their access to their village. Even in an attempt to tell their narrative of the strike, there is another voice present, one of the state.

However, it is clear that the 'Solo' voice is out of place in the poem: it appears once, consists of only two words, and is then, as Bentley sees it, displaced by the Chorus. In the footnote to the Solo, Bentley also tells us that the 'wankers' comment comes from a 'policeman greeting pickets', which is more information than we are given for any of the subsequent *Thurcroft* quotations that make up the Chorus. In the prominence given to the mining voices against this single voice from the police, the voice of the 'village' comes to drive out the voice of the 'state'. However, Bentley omits any biographical details from any of the appearances of the Chorus. In the retelling of the narrative, the who of the voice has been expunged, it has become a single voice, a contribution to an alternative narrative. The Chorus exists both as the singular voice of a person and the collective voice of a people and place.

There is, however, an ethical concern to be taken into account when considering how Bentley uses these voices in the poem. As Susan Sontag puts it: 'no "we" should be taken for granted when the subject is looking at other people's pain' (2003, 6). Bentley seems aware that pain does not disappear, but that it shifts and becomes something else. The passage of time between the miners' strike of 1984–5 and Bentley's *Largo* means that the pain Bentley represents is a pain that no longer exists in the same form as it once did. It is a pain engendered by a lack of representation and a loss of voice, rather than the hardships of the strike itself.

Although Bentley's 'Chorus' exists as both singular and collective, the quotations taken from Thurcroft do privilege a 'we'. This 'we' comes from the people of the village itself—*'this time we did say something'* (Bentley 2011, 12). 'We' is the term by which the people of Thurcroft have chosen to represent themselves. John Berger says that 'poetry can repair no loss but it defies the space which separates. And it does this by its continual labor of reassembling what has been scattered' (2005, 95). Bentley's use of the voices of Thurcroft does not take their struggle for granted or fail to appreciate the villagers' individual labours during the strike; Bentley's appropriation is an attempt to defy the space that has been established between the marginalised voices of the people of Thurcroft (and more broadly the working classes) and the 'official' strike narrative of 1984–5. Bentley's poem draws the voices from *Thurcroft* into conversation with his poem and its conversation with contemporary labour issues and strike narratives. Poet Natasha Sajé claims that 'poems that deal with the lives of others need to show an awareness (which may be implicit as well as explicit) that another person is always a complicated story' (2009, n.pag.). Bentley's splicing together of various literary and cultural reference points in 'The Two Magicians', as well as the voices of the people of Thurcroft, shows him to be a writer engaged with and performing these complications in the poem. The voices from Thurcroft are not inserted into 'The Two Magicians' to simply provide authentic, working-class strike voices, but to help establish a narrative (and poem) that refuses to conceal the complications that arise in the construction of our labour histories.

In terms of the Chorus, Bentley constructs and uses its collective and singular voice to demonstrate the ways in which strike and union narratives come to be formed and manipulated. In music, a chorus is that which constitutes a return, a repetition and a (re)focusing on the song's main idea or concept. In 'The Two Magicians', while the source material, *Thurcroft*, is repeated, the content of each Chorus is not. Unless we see the repetition thematically, in terms of collective struggle—*'But this time we did say something'* (Bentley 2011, 12). In *Thurcroft*, the 'voices' change. In the poem, while the words change, the 'voices' stay the same. What Bentley does, by appropriating the speech as a Chorus, is to frame the singular instance as a representation of the larger collective struggle during the strike. Although it was originally a single voice, Bentley affords each voice the authority to speak for and as a group, highlighting the cooperative effort that necessitates the continuation of any strike or political struggle. However, the individual gives way to and is swamped by a collective narrative of place and memory. Bentley allows the village itself to speak, and those residents who speak do so with a single voice, where who said what becomes largely irrelevant. There is a clear understanding that this is a construction of unanimity. The 'village' is distilled in the book *Thurcroft* and then further concentrated in the poem. As 'The Two Magicians' was published in 2011, and the Thurcroft Colliery was closed in 1991, the poem is presenting memories of a place that no longer exists, at least in terms of its 'primary purpose' as a pit village. In one Chorus, a father rhetorically asks his daughter, *'Now you're missing your picketing, aren't you?'* (Bentley 2011, 18). The sense becomes that of a daughter not simply missing the act of picketing itself, but also of having anything to picket for. There is no mine and there are no jobs to protect. In *Thurcroft*, the contributors and editors are attempting to retell the story of the strike in a pit village. Where Bentley repurposes sections of *Thurcroft*, the Chorus becomes the retelling of people remembering a place that does not exist. The Chorus becomes almost an apparition, the italicised text reinforcing the idea that the edges of this story have been blurred, and that we are 'hearing' and looking at a representation of a place that may once have existed.

Thinking of the Chorus in terms that we may traditionally associate with ancient Greek drama—an idea that Bentley said he had in mind when constructing the Chorus—it becomes more than a simple act of representation. In our email correspondence, Bentley said that with the Chorus he 'had the Greek stage in mind, and (very loosely) in regard to Tony Harrison's use of the chorus in his dramatic works'. The link to Harrison comes about in relation to Harrison's 1981 translation of Aeschylus' *Oresteia* and Harrison's 1985 libretto, *Medea: A Sex-War Opera*. While Harrison's *Oresteia* employed an all-male cast for the production in keeping with ancient Greek practice, Harrison's *Medea* separates the Chorus in two, a male and a female chorus. The male Chorus implores the

'State Official' to 'throw the switch / on MEDEA, the child-killing witch', while the female Chorus asks, 'what male propaganda lurks / behind most operatic works / that music's masking?' (1986, 368 and 370). As Steve Padley notes, the Chorus of women

> incisively scrutinises the link between patriarchal and cultural values, the eloquence of their discourse reversing traditional associations of the female with the private speech of the *oikos* against those of the male with the public rational debate of the *polis*. (2001, n.pag.)

While Bentley's Chorus does not perform the same function as the one Steve Padley posits, we can read it, and 'The Two Magicians' as a whole, as challenging some of the notions of 'private speech' alongside 'public debate'. The private utterances of the people of Thurcroft are repositioned and employed to speak as a 'public' alongside Bentley's own, 'private', strike reminiscences. The private narratives are employed as public ones. *Thurcroft* repositions private utterances as public in a way that blurs the line between the two, while the poem then appropriates them for and as poetry. To borrow terms from Padley and Greek theatre, the *oikos* of the individual reminiscences in *Thurcroft* become the *polis* in Bentley's work, while Bentley's own poetry acts as the *oikos* itself.

At the end of section IV of the poem, this blurring is in evidence when Bentley writes:

> The dogs closing in. The trap set.
>   Wham!—they can't see what's coming.
>
> Chorus:
>
> *They saw us and started chasing us back through the wood. We were running*
> *Blind, falling over stumps and running into trees.* (2011, 14)

The section not in italics is Bentley's words, the italicised section has been lifted from *Thurcroft*. Bentley's 'dogs' cross over the demarcation provided by the word 'Chorus' and become part of the 'they' chasing the miners ('us'). Bentley's private strike reminiscences become part of the people of Thurcroft's story. Bentley's own words repurpose and reconsider the words and stories of the people of Thurcroft. Bentley's 'dogs' join the chase, along with the 'riot police with shields, batons and dogs' from *Thurcroft* (Gibbon & Steyne 1986, 89), combining the two narratives into a new rendering of this particular story of the strike. Bentley's words—'Wham!'—are reflected in the strikers—*'running into trees'*—even though Bentley is writing almost thirty years later. The past comes to comment upon the present, and the present creates the space for the past to be reassessed and re-evaluated.

The space in which the Chorus is performed is the private act of reading, while the Chorus is itself performing in and for the poem. It is performing *in* the poem in that the quotations exist as 'visitors' from another piece of work, ostensibly about the same subject, but nevertheless 'tied' to both a physical object—the book, *Thurcroft*—and a physical space and specific time—Thurcroft as town after the miners' strike. The quotations are performing the role of 'visitors' or even 'exiles' from a place, the town of Thurcroft, that no longer functions in its (initial) primary purpose, serving the now closed Thurcroft Colliery. The *Thurcroft* quotations are now serving the needs of Bentley and the poem, so are performing *for* and as a part of the poem's whole. The interviews that the people of Thurcroft gave about Thurcroft and the miners' strike of 1984–5 are no longer solely about Thurcroft and the miners' strike, but also about Bentley's poem and the strike's legacy. The people who gave the interviews no longer have control over them. The narratives of the people of Thurcroft are now part of the strike legacy, a strike legacy that Bentley co-opts for his own poem. They were not Bentley's words initially, but they in effect become his, and part of his contribution to the strike narrative.

The Chorus, when it appears, comes at the bottom of the page and mediates between the poem's past and future (as enacted by the movement from one page to the next). The Chorus comes after the poem 'proper' and as such it becomes almost the product of and, at the same time, a comment on the poem's content. In the Chorus that ends section IV, the rabbits being chased by dogs in the poem 'magick into the miners chased by police through the wood in the Chorus' (Bentley, email correspondence 2 Mar. 2017)—'The dogs closing in. The trap set. / Wham!—they can't see what's coming […] *They saw us and started chasing us back through the wood. We were running blind, falling over stumps and running into trees*' (Bentley 2011, 14). Bentley's use of the phrase 'magick into' prematurely shuts down what appears to happen between these two 'sections' of the poem. The rabbits that are mentioned become the strikers. Yet it would seem that while the rabbits do become the strikers, in the sense that they give way to the strikers as the Chorus begins, this still neglects that both exist on the page, simultaneously. While reading the poem, we are aware that the rabbits exist before we realise that they will become or be reimagined as miners, but we cannot ever read the striking miners of the Chorus without the rabbits. The rabbits are always present in the reading, even when they are not referenced. Our legacies are formed both by explicit reference points and 'stories', and those which have been sidelined or covered over. The Chorus is necessarily indebted to the past, it is a (indirect) product of it in the poem. However, the Chorus also mediates and reconfigures our understanding of the past. It thereby creates a new present and platform for the future.

Visually, the Chorus acts almost as a valve or bridge between the two sections of the poem, a connection between separated voices, places and times. It allows voices to be heard, it establishes a place for them. Bentley himself said: 'I was very conscious of the magnitude of my subject, and felt that my own voice was not adequate to it—that this was a subject that demanded a chorus of voices' (email correspondence 2 Mar. 2017). It is as if the Chorus is the foundation on which the poem is built, or at least that which stabilises it. The Chorus provides the voice of collective experience that gives the poem the validity and authentication Bentley believes it to require. However, the *Thurcroft* utterances are removed from the realm of the 'non-fictional' oral history to a work whose artifice is clearly evident. As we are perhaps encouraged to view the *Thurcroft* sections as 'true', we are in danger of missing the contrived nature of the construction of these legacies in the first instance: first as oral text, then as transcribed oral text and, finally, appropriated to become part of Bentley's poem.

Through the quotations that constitute the various appearances of the Chorus, it seems clear that place functions as a shorthand for wider questions regarding representation. The first two Choruses include brief sections, quoted second-hand from the police, in which questions around how space is controlled and who controls space are explored:

> *We've been through more farms than I could count. Can you imagine creeping through a farmyard at three in the morning trying not to wake the dogs or ducks? Then we'd get out of the car, unlock the gate or lift it off its hinges, and put it back so nobody'd know we'd been through. Then you'd come out and the police'd be round the next corner. 'Where are you going lads?' 'Fishing.' We went 'fishing' a lot. It was cat and mouse.* (Bentley 2011, 10)

The 'voice' from the Chorus draws attention to how the strikers have to exploit and adapt to a place that has been corrupted by state influence. Through the lifting off and replacing of gates, there is the desire to avoid the appearance of having been in the space at all. The strikers are forced into a situation where they become practically complicit in the undermining of their own space and the space of those around them. They are forced to explore alternative or undesirable spaces, after the police have occupied their place—'police waiting round a corner […] pulled over in our place' (Bentley 2011, 10). But yet, the strikers are able to manipulate their own space, demonstrating a connection to the area and understanding of it that is unavailable to those from outside. It is clear that the relationship between the strikers and their place is a fraught one. Yet the Chorus and Bentley attempt to re-establish 'our place'. 'Their car pulled over in our place', the final line of the stanza, leads directly into the Chorus where the voice of the strikers are given the space to deliver the final comment of this section of the poem.

As the strikers, even after their 'creeping' and being forced to navigate alternative routes across other people's land, are nonetheless spotted by the police—a situation which appears to be the norm—their claims to the place are undermined. It is the police (and state) who decide where their place is and how they are to function within it. If the police know where the strikers are going to appear, but show no interest in where they have come from, it stands to reason that the police have allowed the strikers to get as far as they have. It is from the control of space that the police derive their authority: '*They tried to keep us in one spot, so we started walking up and down. One of the inspectors was getting a bit uppity, "You stay there, you say nothing"*' (Bentley 2011, 12). After being kettled, the strikers attempt to regain some of their autonomy through the act of 'walking up and down', thereby occupying and pushing to the boundaries of the place into which they have been forced. The fact that the choruses in the poem are all written in prose, with line breaks dictated by page size, means that the words of the people of Thurcroft begin to fill the space in which they are presented, again as if they are pushing at someone else's borders. Bentley's own 'poetic' sections of the poem 'occupy' space, their position linked to their own creation and publication. Bentley's words have been created for this poem, their place is their own. The narrative he writes is confident in its position as 'occupier'. The Chorus does not have that luxury.

The Chorus is attempting to exist within a place and a time where it is not at home. These voices no longer have the cultural weight to occupy space in the way they did in *Thurcroft*. The police officer's insistence that the strikers 'stay there' and 'say nothing' points to the way in which those who control space can begin to control the voices and the stories we tell. What Bentley is doing is itself a form of controlling these voices. Bentley's inclusion of this phrase from the police highlights the modes through which voices can become marginalised when other voices come to occupy and control the place where these (now marginalised) voices were once heard. Bentley repositions these voices, not to silence them, but to allow them to speak again to a new place and time. As Simon Armitage notes in his book *Walking Home*, whereas 'prose fills a space, like a liquid poured in from the top [...] poetry *occupies* it, arrays itself in formation, sets up camp and refuses to budge' (2012, 5). This is what Bentley is attempting with 'The Two Magicians'. His poem creates a place which is then filled with voices that have been ousted from (or been deprived of) their own place. These voices have a place returned to them, which they are allowed to occupy and from which they can establish a presence to be heard again. Even though these voices are removed from their original setting and their names are 'lost' in Bentley's poem, they are inserted into Bentley's contemporary strike narrative. Their voices are given the opportunity to compete against the dominant narratives that have supplanted them.

II. Helen Mort's 'Scab' and 'Pit Closure as a Tarantino Short' and Steve Ely's 'Objective One'

This final section of this chapter will examine the work of other two poets who have published post-2010 to consider how the legacy of the miners' strike of 1984–5, particularly in the north-east, has come, in part, to be shaped by outside actors.

In *Division Street*, Helen Mort questions how narratives of place, particularly post-industrial and post-strike, are constructed. A quotation from poet Michael Symmons Roberts that appears on the rear cover of the book claims that what underlies the work 'is the bedrock of the north of England, its landscapes and stories'. Roberts's 'bedrock' seems to speak to some essential foundation of the north and its stories, if such a thing could ever exist. Mort presents a north in which this 'bedrock' of the idea(s) of the north, its people and histories has become almost impossible to separate from the cultural products that seek to represent it.

In the poem 'Scab', Mort looks at the way labour narratives of the north-east have come to be appropriated, and what that leaves behind for those people whom these narratives purport to represent. Turning to a section taken from towards the end of the poem:

> Years on, we'll make a blockbuster
> from this: a film that gives the town
> its own brass band, cuts out
> the knuckles fringed with blood,
> grafts in a panorama of the Moors.
> This is our heritage: an actor
> artfully roughed up, thirty years
> of editing to keep the landfills
> out of shot. (Mort 2013, 22)

Mort opens this section with lines that suggest that this loss of recognition affects both time and place: 'Years on, we'll make a blockbuster / from this' (2013, 22). The 'brass band' reference suggests Mort is referring to the 1996 Mark Herman-directed film *Brassed Off*.[4] If we take the 'blockbuster'

---

[4] The film, set roughly ten years after the 1984–5 miners' strike had ended, tells the story of the colliery brass band from the fictional town of 'Grimley'—based on Grimethorpe—and the Coal Board's attempts to shut down the pit. Although

as being *Brassed Off*, we encounter a situation in which a voice from the past is predicting a situation that for us as readers has already come to pass. The voice is already aware that the strike narrative will be constructed by someone else from outside of the mining community. Yet Mort is writing in the early part of the 2010s. Mort's words become a prediction for another, future, 'blockbuster'. The strike stretches backwards and forwards in time, so that ascribing any sense of its beginnings and endings becomes a matter of cultural guesswork. What will the blockbuster be made from: will it be reminiscences of the strike, as in Bentley? Will it be the Jeremy Deller re-enactment and documentary, as discussed in Chapter Two? Will it be Mort's own work? Or will it be some other cultural product completely? It is impossible to gauge exactly from where our labour narratives originate or what they contain.

While Mort says we will make a 'blockbuster', this 'we' is not those involved in the strike. Their heritage is someone else's production. Mort writes of how the 'knuckles fringed with blood' have been 'cut out' and been replaced by an actor 'artfully roughed up'. The reality of the strike has been removed, replaced with a stylisation that provides for a more palatable strike narrative. Even the landscape is stylised with the landfills kept 'out of shot' (Mort 2013, 22). In *Brassed Off*, as a result of the debts and hardships they have been saddled with since the strike's end, the miners vote for redundancy and the closure of the pit. The film ends with the colliery brass band winning a national competition and a sense of hope for the future. The 'landfills' are still there, but there is an encouragement to ignore them, not to see the 'waste' and histories that have been excluded or covered. Mort's 'keep the landfills out' suggests a concern of those making the 'blockbuster' that the landfills will somehow slide back into view. A view that brings with it questions about the north and its past and present that those telling these stories do not wish to confront, a legacy of continuing hardship that does not fit with this 'redemptive' narrative arc.

The words that are used to describe the blockbuster are also the language of traditional labour. Mort's use of 'make', 'brass', 'grafts' and 'cuts', all terms of physical work, here speak to the process of making films. This process is a form of work, but one removed from the manual jobs that these words once represented. There is no longer a (mining) industry for these

> *Brassed Off* is the most likely reference point for Mort's poem, the films *Billy Elliot* (2000), *Pride* (2014) and to a lesser extent *Made in Dagenham* (2010) and *The Full Monty* (1997) show *Brassed Off* to exist within a broader culture of strike and 'strike legacy' film-making. Both *Billy Elliot* and *Pride* deal with questions regarding masculinity and sexuality during the miners' strike. *Made in Dagenham* is about the 1968 Ford sewing machinists' strike and the fight for equal pay. *The Full Monty* is set in the early 1970s, and most characters are former workers in Sheffield's steel trade who have been made redundant as a result of the city's declining industrial output.

words to signal or speak to. These words have now been co-opted for (and by) the 'blockbuster'. If the words used to tell your experiences no longer mean the same thing, then your narratives no longer mean the things they once did. They do not communicate a present you recognise. They now tell a different story. The 'blockbuster' has refashioned the strike narrative to tell stories that, while sounding the same as the ones that have always been told, do not mean the same things. The legacy of the miners' strike is no longer in the hands of those who experienced it, if it ever was.

This appropriation of labour narratives also speaks to employment, and the inadequacy of work following the closure of so much industry in the north-east. While the films *Brassed Off* and *The Full Monty* speak to the issues around finding work for miners and ex-steel industry workers, Mort is showing that what has replaced industry and the jobs that have been created in the aftermath of this decline are unsuitable for those who once 'made' and 'grafted'. These jobs, predominantly in the service industry, while providing an income, albeit precariously, do not replace or replicate the cultural and social status that working in more manual forms of industry would have afforded. These are jobs that in no way compensate for the ones that have been lost. As Owen Jones states,

> as well as being poorly paid, many of the service sectors jobs have a markedly lower status than the manufacturing jobs they replaced. Miners and factory workers had a real pride in the work they were doing. Miners were supplying the country's energy needs; factory workers had the satisfaction of investing skill and energy into making things that people needed. The jobs were well regarded in the community. (2012, 158)

Although Jones may make his assertion a little too strongly, his point is undoubtedly true; the shift from well-unionised, 'constructive' employment to a casualised service sector means not only a drop in status, but a thorough reconfiguration of people's roles within a community. This shift means that one no longer has the same role in constructing these narratives of place, and one's ability to see oneself in these stories is removed. This reconfiguration, or the inability to fully reconfigure oneself in light of this shift, leads to the compromising of one's 'place-identity', that which defines 'who the person is, how he or she is to behave, and what he or she is worth' (Proshansky, Fabian & Kaminoff 2014, 81). Without the ability to affix yourself within the narrative, it becomes vulnerable to manipulation. These narratives have been taken from the people they are supposed to represent. These are media narratives and happy endings that in no way speak to the cultural and economic present.

As discussed in regard to Bentley, what Mort is demonstrating is how those places, and the stories surrounding them that we consider to be our own, are in fact much more vulnerable than we might like to admit. Without recognising our own places, we lose a fundamental aspect of that which gives us the ability to construct meaning for ourselves. In the attempt to construct these meanings, people are forced to rely on conceptions of a place that has fundamentally changed. Their narratives and meanings no longer represent a place they see or recognise themselves in.

Steve Ely makes the point regarding the casualisation of work and the 'Hollywoodisation' of the north-east even more strongly in the poem 'Objective One' by invoking Asos, *Brassed Off*, *The Full Monty* and *Billy Elliot*. Ely talks with no small sense of sarcasm of 'Asos and Next PLC [...] bringing light to parochial darkness, / access, investment, enterprise, jobs: / until sterling collapses', until the point at which

> [...] the provincia flips once more
> to wrecking-ball brownfield bombsite,
> the full monty of dole and dereliction,
> where brassed-off, hand-to-mouth yokels
> are abandoned to dearth and absurdity,
> their eh-bah-gum tutu dreams. (2015, 150)

Ely's 'full monty of dole and dereliction' speaks to show how these filmic depictions of the north-east have become ingrained in the labour narratives of the north. The phrase 'full monty' is not simply the title of a movie, but part of the lexicon for an economically depressed north-east. These films are feeding back into and augmenting the labour narratives of the area. These artful depictions first appropriate, and then supplant, the narratives of those people who actually live with these hardships. The movies, and the narratives they depict, are now part of the north-east's cultural legacy. The strike becomes something that is 'artfully' rendered, the edges and 'realities' of the struggle removed or smoothed out by the outside, all the while being presented as 'our heritage' (Mort 2013, 22). 'Our heritage' serves as both a condemnation of the way the strike and the places in which it took place have come to be portrayed, and a comment on the way 'contextual reconstructions' of any event can be 'passed down to become a tradition' (Carver 1998, 163). The story of the strike passes into common ownership. It becomes a public narrative over which the people it is supposed to represent have no control. The narrative becomes larger than the strikers and the areas in which it was fought, yet not in a way which empowers those who were involved.

It is, however, a particular strike narrative of the north-east. While both Ely and Mort are from the north-east and the region looms large in their writing, it is notable that the 'strike movies' *Pride* and *Made in Dagenham* are not mentioned. *Pride*'s focus on the real-life group Lesbians and Gays Support the Miners and their fundraising efforts to support South Walian mining families and *Dagenham*'s female-led machinists strike in 1968 provide counterpoints to the more heteronormative and/or masculine strike narratives of *Brassed Off* and *The Full Monty*. The focus for Ely and Mort is the north-east, but it is, nevertheless, a version of the north-east strike narrative that is almost solely male and heterosexual.

Mort herself, in the poem 'Pit Closure as a Tarantino Short', poetically creates a future 'blockbuster', while exploring how our stories become compromised. The poem opens with the lines: 'The Suit who pulled the trigger left / […] / *Business Closed* was all it said' (2013, 25). Mort is reframing the strike, but more specifically the Tory party's pit closure programme, in the vein of a Hollywood film, one with only two sides, the villain and the victim.

In *The New Yorker*, film critic Richard Brody writes of the director Quentin Tarantino that 'the world that he imagines and admires, one without reconciliation, is essentially and crudely adolescent, a version of history as blood feuds in which anger begets anger and revenge breeds revenge as he watches from the superior position of the cinematic referee, at a safe historical distance' (2012, n.pag.). In 'Scab', the 'knuckles fringed with blood' have been cut out and replaced by an 'artfully roughed up' actor, while here they have both been supplanted by the stylistically excessive violence of a Tarantino movie. This 'movie' is not the comedy-drama of *Brassed Off* or *Billy Elliot*, but something altogether more troubling. By reimagining the pit closure as a Tarantino movie, the 1984–5 strike and the decimation of the mining industry are presented as a 'history of blood feuds' and 'revenge'. From this superior position, the 'cinematic referee', the omnipotent constructor of this crude narrative, is able to exclude the complexities and political and labour circumstances that led to both the pit closures and the strike of 1984–5.

The end of the 'Pit Closure' reads: '*Nothing's finished, only given up.* / Before he left, he checked the lock' (Mort 2013, 25). Mort's 'given up' adds a sense of surrender, along with something being relinquished. The struggles and the legacy of the pit closures are not finished, their impact is still being felt, but the narratives that are being told have been parted with. These stories have been surrendered and what they will be replaced by is almost a satire of the miners' strike. These stories are told by people from the outside who only see the narrative potential of the strike. Although it is the state which destroyed the mining industry over a period of years and the 1984–5 miners' strike only lasted 12 months, in 'Pit Closure' it is reduced to a single, violent act. This act is symbolic of the whole, but it presents the legacy of the miners' strike as a solitary scene, a scene that positions the miners and their families as victims. It is a performance of a history. The violence obscures the struggles, both historic and ongoing, faced by miners, their families and those working in the industrial north-east.

The story is not finished, but it is 'given up' to others to continue with, to continue a legacy or to adopt as their own. As Doreen Massey says, 'the identity of places is very much bound up with the histories which are told of them, how these histories are told, and which history turns out to be dominant' (1995, 186). In 'Scab', Mort questions the happy ending model of *Brassed Off* and strike movies. In 'Pit Closure as a Tarantino Short', she satirises the way in which the 1984–5 strike has come to be seen for its narrative potential, its ability to shock and entertain. This hyper-stylised strike narrative works to expose how labour narratives are manipulated and how they are told (and sold) to the public.

Through all this, Mort shows the danger of narratives that re-establish the concerns of the strike, particularly in the minds of a wider public, in a fashion that allows the story of the strike to be taken away from those who lived it. 'Thirty years of editing' has taken place, both erasing and inserting scenes and characters into the narrative, to the point where one is confronted solely by edits of past edits. In a similar fashion to the book *Thurcroft* and the Bentley poem, these edited texts themselves become vulnerable to appropriation. The 'heritage' becomes unrecognisable as a representation of the place and the people it supposedly portrays. These acts of rendering can become so removed from their source that the politics which the original act was supposed to highlight are lost or buried beneath the drive to entertain.

Yet, aware of these contradictions, it is still impossible to ignore the part that these retellings have in attempts to confront and challenge the legacy of the miners' strike of 1984–5. These retellings are inextricably tied up in the conceptions and narratives of the places about which these poets write. Bentley's poem provides a place for those voices which have become excluded from strike narratives, giving them a place in which to re-establish themselves and to challenge dominant narratives. For Mort and Ely, these voices have already been supplanted. They draw attention to the way in which the films present strike narratives that in no way reflect or speak to the social or economic present of the north-east. These narratives do not empower those living with the reality of industrial decline, they exclude them.

CHAPTER FIVE

Other Poetic Responses

> I send you a *sonnet*. I do not expect you to publish it, but you may show it to whom you please.
>
> Percy Bysshe Shelley, *Letters Vol. 2* (1964)

The previous chapters have looked at how two generations of poets have responded to and shaped strike narratives. Those poems call into question the nature of industrial dispute narratives by foregrounding the selective means by which they are constructed. With this chapter, the focus shifts to consider two 'official' poetic responses to the 1984–5 miners' strike: the National Union of Mineworkers-published collection of miners' poetry *Against All the Odds*, and the poet laureate Ted Hughes's poem 'The Best Worker in Europe'. *Against All the Odds* (1984) is a poetry of witness, written by those involved in the strike, while Hughes's poem, broadcast on the *Today* programme in March 1985, is part of the 'institutional' poetic response to the strike. By considering these two ends of the poetic spectrum, this chapter will explore how these poetic responses attempt to establish strike narratives of 1984–5, before a legacy had come to crystallise.

I. *Against All the Odds*

Against All the Odds is unique in being the only poetry collection to be published by the NUM during the 1984–5 strike—and the only collection to have ever been published by the union, although its official magazine, *The Miner*, published individual poems from time to time.[1] Along with poetry readings, the collection was one of the ways the union chose to

---

[1] Maurice Jones, the editor of *The Miner* between 1982 and 1989, also wrote the foreword to *Against All the Odds*.

fundraise during the 1984–5 strike.[2] Money raised from postal sales of the book went to the NUM's centralised Miners' Hardship Fund, while local miners' support groups could buy copies at reduced prices that could then be 'resold in aid of local funds' (Jones & Ross 1984, 52).

The role of poetry, and *Against All the Odds* in particular, can be seen as a way for writers (both professional and not) to articulate an experience. It was a way of creating a sense of community, not necessarily or solely a poetic one, but one of shared (yet unique) experience and struggle.

In his 1987 essay 'Making History: Writings from the British Coalfields', John Field sees the publication of just a single collection of poetry by the NUM as a missed opportunity:

> Official labor movement organizations, in Britain at least, are unaware of the potential of cultural practice—oral, musical, dramatic and written—to go beyond running commentary on the boss or *ad hoc* fund raising, and move toward construction of a wider class struggle. (1987, 137)

While the NUM's purpose in publishing the collection may have been 'ad hoc fund raising', those who contributed to the collection clearly saw their contribution differently. In the 'Foreword' to the collection, Maurice Jones anticipates the work of future critics and scholars and shows a self-consciousness about the historical significance of the volume as testimony:

> In the years to come historians and analysts will give their endless judgements on the strike of '84, trying to grasp the essence of the people who took part and supported this most titanic of labour struggles. We believe the essence is captured in these poems. (1984, 1)

Jones knows that the strike is a defining moment in late twentieth-century British history, but he situates the collection as one of people's 'essence', rather than ideas. While the strike is ongoing, you support the people who are striking. The NUM is not mentioned at all by Jones. The collection is about the '150,000 striking miners and their families' (Jones 1984, 1) and about establishing strike narratives and capturing strikers' voices. Yet, as Field says, after producing *Against All the Odds*, the NUM 'showed no lasting interest in the remarkable cultural growth that this represented' (1987, 137).

---

[2] During the 1972 miners' strike, poet Tom Pickard had organised a poetry reading at the University of Newcastle 'for the benefit of the miners striking against the Tory government's wage restrictions' (Duncan & Mottram 2007, 71). The other poets involved in the reading included Tony Harrison and Barry MacSweeney.

Other Poetic Responses

Against All the Odds occupies a position of immediacy that the mainstream publication market did not adopt. The book itself was published in September 1984, roughly six months into the strike, and six months before its disheartening end.[3] Being published by the NUM means that the poems in the collection comprise an almost union-sanctioned (poetic) response to the strike, as it was ongoing. One of the first 'poetic responses' to the miners' strike of 1984–5, Tony Harrison's 'V.', was published in November 1985, roughly nine months after the strike's conclusion. *Against* is expressly a response to and about the 1984–5 miners' strike. It is poetry from the 'front line', poetry written in response to an event that had yet to end, a poetry of witness. The poems included in the book are about the struggle and the experience of the miners' strike, not its legacy. Shirley Dent, in the *Guardian*, said of the collection that 'collectively it has two strengths: raw anger and a sense of history in the making' (2009). The poems see the strike as historic, but they also paint its success as near inevitable. Eileen Reddish's 'England—1984' proclaims that 'the miners will win' and that they'll win because they are 'right' (1984, 5). This is poetry as a stimulus and encouragement for continued support. The poems are written by people who want to believe, or make others believe, that the strike is going well. These are poems to rally.

Let us turn to the first poem in *Against All the Odds*, Bill Simms's 'To a Bottom One', which I will quote in full:

> All the miners in the land,
> Your forefathers fought for you.
> Our turn now to make a stand,
> Return their favour true.
>
> All the miners in the land.
> Would wish to keep their jobs.
> So lend your brother a helping hand.
> And picket with the Kens and Bobs.
>
> All the miners in the land,
> Know stocks are wearing thin
> Like a timer shedding sand -
> The bottom one would win.
>
> All the miners in the land,
> Together we'll win the day.

---

[3] September 1984, coincidentally, was also the month in which the strike was declared 'officially' illegal by the high court, as a result of the NUM's 'failure' to hold a national ballot on the proposed strike action.

Other Poetic Responses

> Whatever may the Tories plan,
> The Union's here to stay. (1984, 2)

This being the opening poem of the book, it becomes something of a placeholder, staking a claim for the collection as a whole. The refrain which opens each stanza by calling to 'All the miners in the land' acts as a rallying cry. The poet calls to those miners out on strike, those becoming disheartened by a seemingly unending dispute and those around the UK not on strike. It is their work as miners that binds them first and foremost and, with the repetition of the line, it is in these terms that they should see themselves. What this line does, particularly when coupled with the ABAB rhyme scheme that Simms employs, is set up an 'us' and 'them' dynamic— the miners as 'us', and a 'them' which includes both the Tories and to an extent the general populace. There is a clear notion of the audience to whom this work is addressed: other miners and their families.

The first stanza of Simms's poem plays to other miners' sense of a shared history to situate the strike within a lineage of industrial action. The poem recalls the miners' 'forefathers' and their struggles, and asserts that it is the current miners' turn to repay the 'favour'. Mining is presented not as a choice, but as a family business, a tradition: mining not just as the job that an individual worker does, not simply a form of employment, but as a (familial) history of working-class struggle itself. It is, however, a history which is wholly male.

The terms in which Simms writes are unambiguous: it is the language of conflict. However, the previous miners' strike having taken place only ten years before the strike of 1984–5, Simms's 'forefathers' are also many of the miners' younger selves. It is not just to previous generations that the miners of the 1984–5 strike owe a debt, but to themselves, to continue to protect all they had fought for just a decade before. This is an industry contending with its own history. This history, particularly in the context of recent (and repeated) disputes between workers and the Tory government, is one that at least needs to be acknowledged. The refrain calls backwards to those who have been on strike and fought for workers' rights over generations, and forwards to those who will be affected and shaped by the legacy of the 1984–5 miners' strike, and the wider context of industrial decline in the UK. Yet, without the refrain, its constant repetition, its reinforcement of an idea, its refusal to go quietly, there is the underlying concern that the miners' message and their history is liable to be lost or simply forgotten.

'To a Bottom One' is hardly an anomaly within the collection. The concerns with history, family and the 'them' and 'us' dynamic between the miners and the Tory government are present throughout the book. *Against All the Odds* contains over forty poems, with Bill Ross, one of the editors, being the only contributor to have more than one entry. Ross's two poems are outliers, poetic eulogies for two miners, David Jones and Joe Green, who died during the first few months of the strike.[4] J. McMillan's 'They'll Never Smash the NUM' and R. Colens's '1984' call on the workers to 'unite' behind the NUM against the 'fools who cross the picket line' (McMillan 1984, 17). These are the only poems that explicitly reference the NUM—with Scargill himself only being invoked on a handful of occasions. This is about the strikes. The name that appears most frequently throughout the collection is that of the Chairman of the National Coal Board, Ian MacGregor, whose job it was to drastically reduce the size of, and reliance on, the coal industry in the UK—'Ian MacGregor under contract, / Assigned to the Coal Boards for political impact, / Crushing unions, axeing jobs his profession' (Roberts 1984, 44). Second to MacGregor is Margaret Thatcher, the person who put him in the post—'Maggie Thatcher—Iron Lady / Very clever and very shady' (Roberts 1984, 44).

However, all of these figures are secondary to what seems to be the collection's driving concern, that of honouring the history of labour activism, mining and mineworkers and the impact the strike would have on future generations. There are poems that reference the General Strike of 1926—'The Big Fight' and 'Black Leg'—and others that invoke the Tolpuddle martyrs—'150 Years On' and 'Tolpuddle, July 1st. 1984: The Red Balloon'.[5] The poems are a way of situating the 1984–5 strike as part of a legacy of industrial struggle in the UK, but also a way of glorifying the role the miners have played in the UK's political history—'The second war began, / And suddenly the miners, / Were heroes to a man' (Davitt 1984, 11). There is the suggestion of a debt that is owed to those who had been sent 'down that hell hole' and yet 'took the blows and kicks, / When the miners were defeated, / In Nineteen-twenty-six' (Davitt 1984, 10). However, most affecting are the voices of children in some of the poems and those poems written to children. These are often written by women in the collection.[6] Whether it is the child asking, 'why is Daddy crying,

---

[4] Jones died on 15 March 1984 'amid violent scenes outside Ollerton Colliery'. Green was crushed by a lorry while out picketing in Ferrybridge, West Yorkshire, dying on 15 June 1984 ('Dead Miners "Never Be Forgotten"' 2009). The taxi driver David Wilkie, who was killed when a concrete post was dropped on his car by two striking miners as he took a strike-breaking miner to work, died on 30 November 1984, a few months after the collection had been first published.

[5] The Tolpuddle martyrs were a group of Dorset farmers arrested in 1834 for swearing a secret oath of membership to the Friendly Society of Agricultural Labourers. These 'friendly societies' were essentially a form of 'insurance' for workers: members would pay into the society and receive money back if they were ever taken sick or ill. The six 'martyrs' were sentenced to be sent to Australia. However, they were eventually pardoned and returned to the UK in 1839.

[6] Many of the poems have only the first initial of the writer's first name, so it is impossible to discern who wrote them.

Other Poetic Responses

Mam?' in 'Tell it to the Children' (Walker 1984, 28) or a father saying he 'won't sit back and watch' his son 'signing on the dole' (Jenkins 1984, 47), there is a sense that the miners are fighting for their children's futures, but also their communities at large. There is a fear that the miners and their families are not being heard, that they are 'the silent majority' (O'Cofaigh 1984, 39). There is an awareness of the working class as a majority, but one becoming politically and socially silenced. The concerns with history and legacy are a way of remembering where the writers come from, while the children represent a form of anxiety about the future and a loss of voice in the telling of their own narratives. In some regards, Helen Mort and Paul Bentley themselves are these children now grown up and their strike poems are an attempt to make sense of these legacies.

It is this fear of a loss of history and voice that Katy Shaw invokes when she states that

> Strikers' poetry highlights the written word as a site for the struggle over the legitimacy of the authority of reality, encouraging twenty-first century readers to confront and acknowledge those denied authority, authorship—the right to communicate an account of conflict—and to question the significance of the forms in which accounts are recorded. Significantly, strikers' writings challenge common presumptions about what exactly constitutes historical evidence. (2012, 11)

Strikers' poetry is for Shaw another space in which these 'struggles' may be fought, a space in which the right to contend with and contest those accounts that have sought to silence or exclude strikers' voices and realities can be recorded and heard. One of the works Shaw draws from is Jean Gittins's *Striking Stuff* (1985). (Again, proceeds from this book went directly to the miners' relief fund.) In this collection, Gittins adopts various 'strike' voices, from miners, to pickets, to children of miners, in order to critique attitudes regarding community and structures of institutional power—'A Yorkshire picket / What we do for love, they're doing for th' pay' (Gittins 'The Yorkshire Picket Song').

In 'The Yorkshire Picket Song', Gittins's use of dialect works as a challenge to the strike narratives that were being formed and, indirectly, as a promotion of northern English 'as the language of collective action, of honesty, of long-term gain'. This advocacy is set against what Claire Hélie sees as Gittins's positioning of Standard English as 'the language of lies, individualism and short-lived gains' (Hélie 2015, 9). In the poem, each verse starts with the lines 'Ah'm a picket / A Yorkshire picket' (Gittins 'The Yorkshire Picket Song'). The picket in each instance affirms their position, not as miner or worker or union member, but as someone on the picket line. It is in the act of picketing, at least during the 1984–5

Other Poetic Responses

strike, that Gittins sees these people's representation. Here, being on strike is positioned as action. The miners are not simply removing their labour by not working, they are repurposing that 'labour' through the act of picketing. It is not just miners that Gittins is invoking here. While to be on strike one must be an employee, to picket one needs only to be present and defend the cause. The speaker of the poem is '*a* yorkshire picket'; they are part of a community, one bound through place and the language spoken by those who live there.

In a footnote to the poem, Gittins says that she wrote 'The Yorkshire Picket Song' when the media were presenting miners and their families as 'sub-human morons' and that she 'wanted to say something for [her] "youngest"' who was a regular 'flying picket'. As Stephenson and Spence write, 'despite their marginality in the mining industry, women from mining families played a central role in supporting strike activism' (2012, 1). While Gittins's work does do this, it is bigger than Stephenson and Spence put forward; it is itself also a form of activism. Gittins's writing does not simply support activism, her work is both activism and an attempt at articulating what it means to engage in activism—'so you see, its not exactly for the pay' ('The Yorkshire Picket Song'). If the state seems to have 'made new rules for 1984' that would paint strikers, picketers and miners' families as 'a ruthless, mindless mob' or a 'band of villains, out to break the law', then Gittins's poetry says that this is not the only version of the 1984–5 strike that the public are going to hear ('The Yorkshire Picket Song').

In 'Why Mam, Why?', Gittins not only defends her miner son but seems to suggest that, for her, 'maternal responsibility for informing the young becomes a wider class-based maternalism patiently outlining the terms of reference for an uninformed public' (Stephenson & Spence 2012, 9). Gittins sets the first two lines of each verse as a strike-inflected question from a child to 'mam'—'Why don't the wheels go round mam? / Why don't the wheels go round?' She has said that 'Why Mam' was the first poem she wrote about the strike (Gittins, 'Why Mam, Why?'). The apparent naivety of the daughter's questions—'Why does me dad hate scabs, mam? / Why does me dad hate scabs?'—reveals concerns about a society where these questions need to be answered. The fear is that the strike and those who fought for their jobs and communities are being forgotten by the narrative of the strike. Gittins is also speaking to those who would, wilfully or not, dismiss or misunderstand the nature of the 1984–5 strike and what was at stake—'They have no compassion for you and I / Let our children starve, and the pickets die'. The lack of understanding of the strike present and concern for what the future may become is established in this very first of Gittins's strike poems. The answers that the narrator gives are not for the child asking these questions though. These responses are for a Britain that refuses to hear them.

Other Poetic Responses

Katy Shaw wrote of Gittins's work, in the online newspaper *The London Economic* that 'home-life and working-class culture are put in direct competition with an active, participatory social life' (2015, n.pag.). 'Home-life' and an active 'social life' need not be binaries, and this is not the case in Gittins's work. In 'A Sad Tale of A Striker's Bride', the bride of the title forgoes her dream wedding, because the strike is called, for 'the Registry Office / with only us Dads and us Mams', but declares that she will support her husband regardless: 'Cause when this lot's ower, ah'm glad ah can say / Well, leastways ah married a man'. Shaw writes that the character of the anonymous bride, through her individual experience, 'is forced to confront the wider strike collective, engaging with a common cause' while also 'placing the political firmly before the personal' (2012, 64). What is overlooked is that the personal is shaped by and made to be the political. Marrying 'a man', a striking miner, is a political statement. Her poetry 'speaks of political and national divisions, it shows that the personal is nothing but political' (Hélie 2015, 7). The political is not placed before the personal, it is part of it.

Carolyn Forché writes, in the introduction to the anthology *Against Forgetting: Twentieth-Century Poetry of Witness*, that 'the poetry of witness reclaims the social from the political and in so doing defends the individual against illegitimate forms of coercion' (1993, 45). Forché's formulation seems more useful than Shaw's in that it sees the social as being inherently political from the start. Previous chapters have looked at what happens after strike narratives have been created and how poetry can come to challenge them, after the fact, after narratives have already experienced these 'forms of coercion'. Gittins's direct involvement with the strike—two of her sons worked at Ledston Luck Colliery—clearly positions her as 'witness'. Gittins and others writing in *Against* are attempting to establish a 'strikers' narrative', as the realities of the strike are unfolding, and at the same time as 'official' narratives are being created by the state.

II. The Poet Laureate—Ted Hughes's 'On the Reservations' and 'The Best Worker in Europe'

While *Against all the Odds* constitutes an almost 'guerrilla' poetic response to national events, there is also the 'official' poetic representative, the poet laureate.

John Betjeman, laureate between 1972 and 1984, was silent on the subject of the miners' strike of 1984–5. This is not a surprise. Betjeman died in 1984 and had not published a full collection of poetry—apart from the anthologies *Church Poems* (1981) and *Uncollected Poems* (1982)—since 1974's *A Nip in the Air*. Added to this, it would be something of a stretch to call Betjeman, bar his championing of Victorian architecture, a political poet. Yet the role of laureate is undeniably political. In the UK, the poet laureate is assigned the role of 'commemorating' events of national importance, when the nation is supposed to share a united viewpoint. However, as these events are often royal in nature—engagements, births, marriages and deaths being high on the list—'national importance' is linked to the monarchy. Andrew Motion said, at the end of his tenure in 2009, that over the ten years he had been laureate, 'the old sense of "them" and "us", establishment and avant-garde, London and regions, [had] matured into a curiosity that [was] willing to cross old boundaries' (Motion 2009, n.pag.). However, before Motion reshaped the role of the laureate, it was still one of deference.

In the case of Ted Hughes, who took over the laureateship from Betjeman in December 1984, his relationship with Sylvia Plath, her suicide, his marital infidelities, claims of domestic abuse and his 'response' to her poetry in 1998's *Birthday Letters*, have come to overshadow some other facets of his work and life. In the Elaine Feinstein biography of Hughes, Hughes's 14-year tenure as laureate is dealt with in six pages. The year that encompassed the 1984–5 miners' strike occupies less than a page. The strike, Scargill and Thatcher are not to be found anywhere in the book. Jonathan Bate's *Ted Hughes: The Unauthorised Life* (2015) does include a chapter entitled 'The Laureate' but, again, the miners' strike is not mentioned in any form. For those who would write about Hughes, the strike is simply not a feature.

Feinstein notes that Hughes accepted the position of laureate 'all the more readily because he already believed that there was a close connection between the role of poet and the symbolic place of royalty in society' (2001, 217). The role of poet and of royalty that Feinstein suggests positions them, not necessarily as actors themselves within a political and social landscape, but as illustrative examples of forms of society. Bate says that Hughes 'enjoyed writing Laureate poems' and that 'with his belief in poet as shaman of the tribe and the royal family as embodiment of the land, he took the role more seriously than any of his twentieth-century predecessors' (2015, 429). While poet laureates may not have an effect on governance or how society or policy is shaped directly, they are a symbol or guide—at least during Hughes's tenure. The laureate is not a voice of the people, it is a voice coming from above of how society should respond to events of national importance.

In terms of strikes and labour, in 1984 Hughes wrote the poem 'On the Reservations', in which he reimagines northern miners as the oppressed Native American peoples—'tribally scarred (stitch-tattoos of coal-dust)' (2005, 776). This work was not published until 1988, a number of years after the strike had ended, before later being collected in 1989's *Wolfwatching*. In a letter from 1989, Hughes writes of the poem that:

Other Poetic Responses

> The Reservations are now the superfluous Northern proletarian millions—released from the slavery of the lives that created them (their heroic labours to stay alive) but with nowhere to go, nothing to do etc, in a land occupied by 'the enemy'. That's how they feel & that's more less how they are. Paid by the State//to evaporate. (2007, 566)

The letter from Hughes to his old friend Lucas Myers seems to position 'Reservations' as a poem of anger, an anger directed at those who had cast aside a northern industrial workforce that they both 'created' and exploited. When the letter was written in October 1989, the Thatcher government was still in power, although just over a year later she would resign from her position as Prime Minister and leader of the Conservative Party. The first section of the poem, 'Sitting Bull on Christmas Morning', opens with the lines:

> Who put this pit-head wheel,
> Smashed but carefully folded
> In some sooty fields, into his stocking?
> And this lifetime nightshift—a snarl
> Of sprung celluloid? (Hughes 2005, 776)

The title of the poem and the reference to Sitting Bull suggests that Hughes sees the state as an occupying force in the north. But with the reference to the Christmas 'stocking', he also suggests that the north and its people are expected to be almost grateful for the 'gift' of jobs that had 'scarred' them and the land.

As with Betjeman, perhaps to challenge Hughes on these political terms is undeserved. However, the public platform that the laureateship provides means that there is an argument to be made for this challenge. Sean O'Brien writes that while Hughes shows an interest in poets such as the Serbian Vasko Popa and the Hungarian Jáos Pilinsky—Eastern Bloc poets who 'knew that the least utterance, however carefully encoded, is political'—'for the most part Hughes' "one story" leaves alone, or avoids, or is uninterested by the developing social and political reality of the British Isles in his adult lifetime' (O'Brien 1998, 36–7).[7] Yet it seems undeniable that the act of accepting the laureateship is itself intensely political. As laureate, your work comes to be read through a social and political reality for which you are the official poetic spokesperson. When Hughes was offered the

---

[7] By 'one story', O'Brien is referring to what he sees as Hughes's interweaving factors of 'the natural world and its mythic function' to create the 'one story' which appears to have provided Hughes with 'an apparently bottomless well of material' (1998, 37).

laureateship by Margaret Thatcher, he claimed that he felt as if he'd 'walked into a pit trap' and that 'refusing invoked as many demons as accepting' (2007, 495).[8] The 'pit trap' seems simply coincidental and not a nod towards the miners' strike that was occurring at the time. Nevertheless, to be offered the laureateship in the midst of the strike suggests that Hughes was not viewed as a poet who would be critical of the government. In his letters, the 'demons' Hughes mentions are not made explicit, but they seem to have more to do with the public role that being laureate would undoubtedly bring. Hughes felt that Philip Larkin, who Hughes believed had already been offered and subsequently rejected the laureateship, would have had the 'level-headedness to refuse' the 'infinite little silly problems' that came with the position, which Hughes himself did not (2007, 495). Later in the same letter, Hughes claimed that he had been sent over seven hundred letters and that the primary issue around the laureateship was that

> Every third letter there's a request. Problem is, most people think of the Poet Laureate's role as a public convenience (it's the job's one inconvenience). They don't know yet that things have changed. (2007, 496)

It is unclear what Hughes saw as having changed in the role. The letter, tongue in cheek as it appears to be, suggests that by and large the job of laureate for Hughes was in no way a 'convenient' one, and one that the public, at least to Hughes's mind, did not understand. He was undoubtedly aware of the 'peculiarity' that comes with being laureate and the 'public' role that he had taken on:

> This new life as Laureate has its strangeness. What is most strange of all is the role I now play in the rusty locked-up heart of the Anglo-Saxon common man [sic] woman and child. Very peculiar. (Hughes 2007, 497–8)

The reach of Hughes's poetry was greater than ever before; it was now part of the world of the 'common' man in a way that it previously hadn't been. While the 'rusty locked-up heart' isn't the most endearing description of the 'common' person, there is a comprehension, if not also a certain element

---

[8] Obviously, Hughes did accept the position. Perhaps, as he states, his decision had something to do with 'performing one of [his] mother's wildest dreams' (2007, 496). Jonathan Bate writes that when thinking over the pros and cons of becoming laureate, Hughes called his sister and agent, Olwyn, and while she 'refrained from pressing him', she did remark 'that acceptance would be good for his American sales' (2015, 418).

of apprehension of his new position beyond poetry. It is worth noting that poetry is not mentioned at all. In the letter Hughes continues:

> Everything I come out with is either (a) a megaphone blast from the peak of a mountain of soap-boxes (b) possibly the solution to the whole problem (c) an infinite sum drawn on infinite credit. So I have to be careful what inanities I come out with. (2007, 498)

He is talking about his life as a poet and writer as much as anything else, but there is a clear sense that he is under scrutiny as laureate that he simply never had to entertain as 'poet'. While he is clearly joking about the 'inanities' he comes out with, Hughes makes the point that his writing is now public, whether he wants it to be or not, and that he cannot necessarily control the types of readings that will become attached to his work, and life. His poetry has the potential to be mobilised in a way that means speaking to or about political issues becomes fraught.

In a tongue-in-cheek solution to the problems of his newly politicised position, Hughes says, 'it's best if I now become a silent recluse [...] and never write another word. So my capital will remain unsquandered & my interest will accrue' (2007, 498). While clearly a joke, Hughes is pointing to the pressures of writing, or more specifically publishing, now he is laureate. The joke is that by saying nothing he can't harm his 'stake' as poet and as public figure; it is through silence that one's influence 'accrues', while voicing opinions can be damaging. In 1985, Hughes did publish 'Rain-Charm for the Duchy: A Blessed, Devout Drench for the Christening of His Royal Highness Prince Harry', a poem that only appears to be about the christening of the prince in so much as its title explicitly references it. The original draft of the poem had been written for, but not included in, 1983's *River*.[9]

Hughes made his stance on labour politics more explicit in the poem 'The Best Worker in Europe'. While the poem was written in early 1985, it was uncollected until after Hughes's death. The poem was, as mentioned earlier in the chapter, broadcast on the *Today* programme in March 1985, during the miners' strike.[10] In this poem, Hughes positions a salmon as 'the best worker in Europe'. The poem opens with the lines:

> The best worker in Europe
> Is only six inch long.

---

[9] Jonathan Bate calls 'Rain-Charm for the Duchy' 'a very good poem' which instantly achieved 'a standard [Hughes] would never reach again in his Laureate work' (2015, 419).

[10] The poem was also published in a limited edition run of 155 copies by the Atlantic Salmon Trust in 1985.

> You thought he'd be a bigger chap?
>   Wait till you hear my song, my dears,
>   Wait till you hear my song.
>   No Union cries his Yea or Nay.
>   He works for all, both night and day,
>   With neither subsidy nor pay. (Hughes 2005, 697)

The salmon appears an odd choice, not being particularly regarded for its collective spirit or selflessness. Yet this seeming glorification of unpaid work (and the gratuitous side-swipe at unionism) is a troubling one. Hughes is suggesting a form of indentured servitude under the guise of working for 'all'. His 'he works for all' suggests that he sees unions as occluding this form of almost neoliberal individualism, through the control he sees them as having over their own members. It is not the worker who is crying 'yea or nay', it is the union itself. As Danny O'Connor states, 'here is the Poet Laureate publishing a contentious poem in a national newspaper [...] confronting a fractious debate and using the salmon as a symbol' (2016, 150).[11] The salmon as a symbol is at odds with the ethos of the trade union movement. In regard to the 1984–5 miners' strike, the significance of the poet laureate, even a new one, voicing these 'contentious' opinions during the largest post-war industrial and political dispute in Britain puts them on the side of the state.

Paul Bentley, whose 'The Two Magicians' has been examined in this book, calls the laureateship a 'problematic and distorting issue' when considering the work of Hughes, as it obscures the 'key ideological association latent in Hughes's pre-Laureate nature poems—namely: class' (Bentley 2014, 5, 4). Bentley suggests that Tom Paulin and John Lucas in their writing on Hughes in *Minotaur: Poetry and the Nation State* (1992) and *Modern English Poetry: From Hardy to Hughes* (1986), respectively, see Hughes's poetry as having an 'entrepreneurial energy, in keeping with the ferocious free-market ethos of the Thatcher government that appointed Hughes Laureate' (Bentley 2014, 4). This is put rather succinctly by Bentley, although it is also clear that he disagrees with this conclusion. Bentley does admit, in regard to 'The Best Worker in Europe', that 'the fish looks suspiciously like the embodiment of the Tory mantra of enterprise and self-sufficiency, from which everyone supposedly benefits' (2014, 98).

---

[11] The national newspaper that O'Connor refers to is *The Times*. In the same year, Hughes published a celebratory poem for the Queen Mother, 'Little Salmon Hymn', dedicated to her as the 'godmother of the salmon itself' (O'Connor 2016, 150). The 'salmon' dedication to the Queen Mother comes from the fact that she was patron of the Salmon and Trout Association (Hughes 2005, 1216).

Bentley attempts to situate or account for Hughes's views by saying that

> Hughes has been brought to this contemporary position by contemporary debates about government subsidies, uneconomic pits, and the non-democratic National Union of Mineworkers—which had refused to bow to political pressure to hold a national strike ballot. (2014, 98)

While this may be true, Hughes's exclusion of 'The Best Worker in Europe' from his laureate collection, in an apparent attempt to 'put the lid back on this fraught political pressure point' (Bentley 2014, 99), seems only to increase the volume of the Poet Laureate's relative absence from 'contemporary debates'. Bentley comments that

> Hughes might be sorry for the miners, but his old sense of class allegiance—the Tory establishment as an army of occupation—is problematized [in the poem] by his historical distrust of Marxism, in the shape of the NUM's uncompromising Marxist leader Arthur Scargill. (2014, 98)

Hughes's own position on the NUM (and Scargill in particular) is somewhat less clear than Bentley makes it seem, at least in Hughes's letters. Hughes does not mention Scargill by name in the hundreds of letters in Christopher Reid's *Letters of Ted Hughes*. In one of the few that refer to industrial action, sent to Jack Brown, a Labour county councillor from Yorkshire, in November 1982, Hughes writes that: 'I felt disappointed for you in your political impasse up there' (2007, 462). A footnote, written by Christopher Reid in the *Letters of Ted Hughes*, explains that the

> 'political impasse', devastating to such mining communities as Barnsley, was the strike led by Arthur Scargill, president of the National Union of Mineworkers, and the defiance of it by Margaret Thatcher's Conservative government. (Hughes 2007, 463)

The phrase 'political impasse' that Hughes uses, pointing to a form of stasis and lack of progress, would seem to assign a portion of blame to both sides of the argument. In the same letter, Hughes is significantly more explicit in his feelings about 'Tory dominance' and its effect on politics:

> It occurs to me that more and more often the prolonged Tory dominance—the gradual consolidate of the Eton/Oxford/Tory axis in all positions of social influence—is beginning to have a narrowing and shallowing effect on the cultural atmosphere. (2007, 462)

This letter, written only two years before Hughes became laureate, is clear in expressing how Hughes sees the Tory party, and a certain form of political elite more generally, as having a constricting effect on culture in the early 1980s. Even while laureate, Hughes would say in a letter to the poet Michael Hamburger in 1987 that the 'problem, maybe, is that Margaret [Thatcher] can't be frightened' and that 'she's like the general who says "we can afford 25% casualties"' (2007, 538). In 1987, just before the general election in which Thatcher would win a third term, Hughes published in *The Times* a 'poetic contribution' to the election debate. The poem, 'First Things First: An Election Duet, Performed in the Womb by Foetal Twins', attacks Western governments who value economic activity over environmental protection: 'the cost of the Gross National Product is / for trees no leaves / and waters no fish' (Hughes 2005, 730). As Bate writes, the poem

> blamed man's head long obsession with economic growth, and more particularly the policies of Western governments and the regulations of the European Economic Community, for a mountain of wasted butter, for contaminated tap water, leukaemia brought on by pesticides sprayed on fields, and even the phenomenon of cot death. (2015, 425)[12]

While this polemic from Hughes is directed more broadly at 'government' than it is the Conservative Party, Hughes is clearly not pro-Thatcher or pro-Conservative. However, he does not add his voice, the loudest poetic voice of the time, to those voices speaking up and contending with the treatment of the miners and their families during the 1984–5 strike.

The reason for this move into the work of Hughes is designed to show the gap between 'official' narratives and the work being produced by the poets I have focused on. The writers I have examined are attempting to fill, or at least contend with, precisely this gap in official verse culture. The role of the laureate is about commemorating 'occasions', more specifically royal occasions. On the occasion of the miners' strike of 1984–5, the poet laureate Ted Hughes was ambivalent. Even after the event, he was not forthcoming; the poets this book focuses on were. In *Against All the Odds*, the writers are attempting to establish a narrative that is outside of the quantitative assertions of 'how many people were arrested', 'how many lost their jobs' or 'how much did these incidents cost'. There is an attempt in the collection, not necessarily to control the narrative, but to make sure

---

[12] Hughes writes that 'if the cost of a mountain of butter is / poisoned water in your and / Cot-death' and 'if the cost of Gross National Product is / for trees no leaves / for waters no fish [...] Then let what can't be sold to your brother and sister be / released on the third world' (1987, 10).

that there is a narrative voice that comes from a culturally marginalised perspective. For *Against All the Odds*, there is a sense of poetry as an accessible form, one that has an immediacy, one that can be disseminated on the fringes of, and counter to, mainstream narratives. The poetry in this collection is part of an intervention, an intervention that declares that these voices exist and cannot be discounted.

Conclusion

> Poetry can repair no loss but it defies the space which separates. And it does this by its continual labor of reassembling what has been scattered.
>
> John Berger, *And Our Faces, My Heart, Brief as Photos* (1984)

One phrase that reappears through the poems in this work, one that was briefly mentioned in the Introduction, is 'the enemy within'. In 1982, Margaret Thatcher said in regard to the miners and the trade union movement generally: 'We had to fight the enemy without in the Falklands. We always have to be aware of the enemy within, which is much more difficult to fight and more dangerous to liberty' (Thatcher qtd. in Travis 2013, n.pag.). In Harrison's 'V.', Thatcher's words become 'half versus half, the enemies within' (2008, 23), in O'Brien's 'London Road' the narrator says, 'I've seen the enemy within / The ones I left behind' (1987, 29), whereas Bentley's 'The Two Magicians' sees 'something rising towards us on the news. / The enemy within' (2011, 11). The repetition of the phrase demonstrates not simply a thematic link between the works but the way in which certain narratives and legacies become entrenched, and begin to occupy the language through which certain historical events and groups are represented. In 'London Road', published just two years after the end of the 1984–5 strike, O'Brien is already aware of the formation of these legacies in the ones he 'left behind'. Alan Sinfield claims that 'powerful stories—those useful to powerful groups—tend to drive out others' (2007, 28). The phrase from Thatcher has continued, it has been imported into the poem, but the miners, the unions and their legacies have not. It is not simply the miners and their families who have been left behind, it is also their ability to control the way their histories are told and retold. Bentley takes this a step further, for we are not presented with a people 'left behind' at all, it is now a news report which carries Thatcher's message. What persists is this phrase, 'the enemy within'. It may have been slightly altered, it may have been packaged differently, but it is still there.

Charles Bernstein writes that 'poetry can bring to awareness questions of authority and conventionality, not to overthrow them, as in a certain reading of destructive intent, but to reconfigure: a necessary defiguration as prerequisite for refiguration' (1990, n.pag.). While certain union narratives and legacies may dominate, these poems draw attention to the construction and the constructed nature of these narratives. Dominant narratives do not so much 'drive out' others, but rather they attempt to subdue or subsume them. Poems draw attention to their own construction simply through the white space they leave on the page. Simon Armitage writes that poems are arrayed 'in formation' (2012, 5): a formation that is clearly constructed around a series of aesthetic and linguistic choices. These poems are a challenge. 'Poetry engages public language as its roots, in that it tests the limits of conventionality while forging alternate conventions' (Bernstein 1990, n.pag.). What the poems here do, by bringing these dominant narratives onto the page (alongside various reminiscences, retellings and re-enactments of strike histories and legacies), is foreground not simply the constructed nature of the poem but, as a corollary, the constructed nature of the narratives and legacies that have come to dominate discussions surrounding industrial disputes and labour representations.

The three poets that constitute the 'foundation', Barry MacSweeney, Tony Harrison and Sean O'Brien, contend with the strikes not long after they had finished, with the stories of the industrial disputes about which they write already in the process of crystallising.

Harrison writes in 'V.' that 'the unending violence of US and THEM' is 'personified in 1984' (2008, 11). If 1984 has come to represent or embody this notion of violence, then it follows that the narratives surrounding the 1984–5 strike come to be represented in a particular fashion, for this is the material from which these narratives are constructed. Or, it is that the 'official' stories that are already being told foreground this idea of violence, and it is these stories that are instilling (or have instilled) this quality into the year. Harrison says that 'on the late-night national news we see / police v. pickets at a coke-plant gate, / old violence and old disunity' (2008, 30). Harrison is not saying that this 'old violence and old disunity' is simply a long-held antagonism between the pickets and the police (or the workers and the state), but that the way the strike is being reported and presented is through old images and stories. The narrative of the strike is already solidifying. This old disunity is coming to shape and then justify a political present. The official story of the strike is already beginning to take form. O'Brien's 'Summertime' begins with the phrase 'The news is old' and ends by saying *'that kind of thing can't happen here, / And when it does it isn't true'* (1987, 18). The news is 'old' because the story is always the same. If something comes to contradict or challenge this view of the strike or the events of the dispute, it simply 'isn't true'. It is not that these things, these counter-narratives, don't exist, it is that they 'can't happen here'. They can't be allowed to happen, they can't destabilise the narrative. That 'kind of thing' can't happen within the realm of the 'official' narrative, it can only happen in another place, in this case, within O'Brien's poem. In MacSweeney's 'The Shells Her Auburn Hair Did Show', the narrator asks 'what / does a government do? Can it make you speak?' (2003, 204). If the government can make you speak, it can also silence you. By controlling the way stories are told, you shape the way these stories come to be retold. In 'Black Torch Sunrise', MacSweeney writes of newspapers and televisions reporting through their 'suitable captions / of a certain persuasion' (1978, 71). 'Persuasion' doubles as the act through which to convince someone and as a set of political beliefs. While the *Telegraph* happily reports that 'days lost in strikes are the lowest in seven years', the whipping of 'left-bank women students' begins to 'blur on the shimmered screen' (MacSweeney 1978, 71, 72). The narrative is altered, to obscure that which doesn't fit with the 'certain persuasion', the 'official' version of the story. MacSweeney's 'blurring' demonstrates that these alternative narratives cannot be completely eradicated, they are still there, but they are in need of something to bring them into focus. The poems highlight the insidious nature of these stories, and the groups that seek to control the narrative and legacies of industrial relations. Yet these older works are also creating a place in which these narratives can be reconsidered (and exposed), while at the same time contributing to the narratives and legacies that are found in the poems that have been published in the past decade.

In the works of Helen Mort, Steve Ely and Paul Bentley, what we see is an attempt to contend with trade union and strike legacies that have become permeated by decades of narrative and counter-narrative, in a UK in which trade union representation has been declining. Mort's 'Scab' references Jeremy Deller's re-enactment of the Battle of Orgreave, along with the movie *Brassed Off* and her own experiences of growing up in Sheffield and attending university in Cambridge, before the narrator is 'left to guess which picket line [they've] crossed' (2013, 22–3). These strike reminiscences and narratives are portrayed as being so entwined with one another that the legacy of the 1984–5 miners' strike is one of fragments. The 'picket line' is still there, but the terms of the dispute are now unclear. The legacies of the strike have come to supplant the understanding of its origins. The trade unions in the poem are conspicuously absent, their role in the legacies of the strike nullified. 'Scab' ends with the lines 'someone / has scrawled the worst insult they can— / a name. Look close. It's yours' (2013, 22). These lines echo Harrison's 'he aerosolled his name. And it was mine' (2008, 22). Harrison's work is shown to now be part of these legacies. Harrison's reflexive 'mine', a comment on his own role as poet and the legacy of his work at the end of the 1984–5 strike, is reversed by Mort to show how we are all implicated and complicit in curating and continuing these strike legacies and narratives.

In 'The Two Magicians', Bentley fills the space of the poem with 'visitors' from *Thurcroft*, with song lyrics, snatches of canonical poetry, references to television and personal reminiscences, in a fashion that foregrounds the constructed, and occasionally convoluted, nature of our stories and narratives. In the poem, all of these voices come to occupy the space that Bentley has created to tell his strike narrative, yet he has brought them there. Bentley writes that 'all hath suffered change' (2011, 17). It is not simply the people who have lived through the strike, but those affected by its legacy who are part of this change. The voices in the poem compete with, augment and reposition one other, while still being presented as a cohesive whole through Bentley's work. Bentley presents what at first appears a singular strike narrative, highlighting the ways in which our historical narratives can take on the appearance of inevitability and dominant narratives come to be seen as the only narrative. He is exposing the performance that is at the heart of any narrative and cultural legacy. As mentioned earlier, Bentley has said that he thought of the poem 'as a poem of voices—a patchwork of direct quotations, memories, and echoes, stitched loosely onto the old ballad' form. Legacies, particularly in this case of the 1984–5 strike, are neither absolute nor the product of a single voice, they are a 'patchwork' of experiences and cultural products that are (both intentionally and inadvertently) 'stitched together' into a form that enables us to justify, to make sense of, or challenge, a political and cultural present.

For Steve Ely's poetry, 'the past is not past: it is in the present and intrinsic to it; it is how the present came to be' (Pugh 2015, n.pag.). While both Mort and Bentley omit any reference to trade unions in their poems, and only include passing reference to either Margaret Thatcher or Arthur Scargill, the unions and the figures that come to represent them are at the heart of Ely's poems. Whereas Mort and Bentley seem to see the narrative of the 1984–5 strike as no longer including (or having space for) trade unions, Ely sees unions and the history of industrial struggle as intrinsic to understanding the political and labour present. In his poetic history of the NUM and trade union oppression, 'Ballad of the Scabs', Ely writes that 'all those bastards need to win / is Brotherhood to fail' and that the war on the 'state machine' is only 'won by unity' (2015, 139, 142). This 'unity' that Ely writes of is one that comes from the working class being 'prepared to stand and fight' (2015, 139), a fight that is led by a strong union movement. If Bentley's work is a 'patchwork' of different voices that exist alongside one another, Ely's voices are openly antagonistic. Be it through his 'Theatre of Hate' in the playlet 'Nithing', the battle between Arthur Wellesley and Peter Mandelson for the attentions of the 'swinish multitude' in 'Scum of the Earth' or the imagined *Question Time* face-off between Arthur Scargill and Cecil Parkinson, Ely's voices compete for space and attention. Ely's work presents the narratives surrounding trade unions as actively under threat from the state and 'official' narratives. Ely's work raises the voices of the unions and the working classes, not always in a way that is comfortable or comforting, to allow them to take up arms against these dominant legacies that seek to exclude them.

The exploration of strike narratives and legacies in this book has endeavoured to show that the weakening of trade unions was a decision. It was a decision taken by a ruling class that sought to blunt the political power of the working classes. It was a choice. This state-sponsored drive to weaken unions in the UK was carried out, in part, through a concerted effort to control the narratives and stories that are told regarding strike action and labour politics. Yet, 'not for the first time, poets have declined to say what politicians would like to hear' (O'Brien 2003, 571). What these poems do is speak to labour narratives. The decline in trade union representation in the UK has led to a crystallisation of the narratives that surround industrial action and union legacies. These poems remind us of how narratives and legacies are formed, and make it possible to see how they may be rewritten.

Bibliography

'1972: Miners Call Off Crippling Coal Strike'. *BBC News.* 2015. Web. Accessed 20 Dec. 2015.

Abercrombie, Nicholas, and Alan Warde. *Contemporary British Society.* Cambridge: Polity, 1988. Print.

'About the TUC'. Tuc.org.uk. 2015. Web. Accessed 2 Nov. 2015.

Alexander, Elizabeth. 'Praise Song for the Day'. Poets.org. 2009. Web. Accessed 30 May 2018.

Amis, Martin. *The War against Cliche: Essays and Reviews 1971–2000.* London: Vintage, 2002. Print.

Armitage, Simon. *Walking Home: Travels with a Troubadour on the Pennine Way.* London: Faber and Faber, 2012. Print.

Aronowitz, Stanley. *The Death and Life of American Labor.* London: Verso, 2014. MOBI File.

'Arthur Scargill Loses London Flat Case'. *BBC News.* 2012. Web. Accessed 14 Nov. 2016.

Aspinall, Arthur. *The Early English Trade Unions.* London: Batchworth Press, 1949. Print.

Astley, Neil. 'The Riff-raff Takes Over'. *V.* Northumberland: Bloodaxe, 2008: 35–6. Print.

Auden, W.H. 'In Memory of W.B. Yeats'. *Selected Poems.* New York: Vintage, 1979: 80–3.

Batchelor, Paul. 'I Am Pearl': Guise and Excess in the Poetry of Barry MacSweeney. Doctoral thesis. University of Newcastle, 2008. Web. Accessed 24 Jul. 2018.

Bate, Jonathan. *Ted Hughes: The Unauthorised Life.* London: William Collins, 2015. Print.

Battersby, Eileen. 'The Politics of Poetry'. *Irish Times.* 1996. Web. Accessed 28 Aug. 2018.

'"Battle Of Orgreave": Probe into 1984 Miners' Clash Policing Ruled Out'. *BBC News.* 2016. Web. Accessed 10 Mar. 2016.

Beckett, Andy. *When the Lights Went Out.* London: Faber, 2009. Print.

Beckett, Francis, and David Hencke. *Marching to the Fault Line.* London: Constable, 2009. Print.

Bibliography

Beharrell, Peter. *Bad News*. London: Routledge and Kegan Paul, 1976. Print.

Bell, Bethan, and Shabnam Mahmood. 'Grunwick Dispute: What Did the "Strikers in Saris" Achieve?' *BBC News*. 2016. Web. Accessed 4 Apr. 2018.

Bentley, Paul. *Largo*. Sheffield: Smith/Doorstop, 2011. Print.

Bentley, Paul. 'The Poetry Business'. Poetrybusiness.co.uk. N.d. Web. Accessed 28 Sept. 2016.

Bentley, Paul. *Ted Hughes, Class and Violence*. London: Bloomsbury, 2014. Print.

Berger, John. *And Our Faces, My Heart, Brief as Photos*. London: Bloomsbury, 2005. MOBI File.

Bernstein, Charles. 'Comedy and the Poetics of Political Form'. *The Politics Of Poetic Form*. New York: Roof, 1990. MOBI File.

Billings, Joshua, Felix Budelmann and Fiona Macintosh. 'Introduction'. *Choruses, Ancient and Modern*. Oxford: Oxford University Press, 2014: 1–14. Print.

Bloodworth, James. *Hired: Six Months Undercover in Low-Wage Britain*. London: Atlantic Books, 2018. MOBI File

Brody, Richard. 'The Riddle of Tarantino'. *The New Yorker*. 2012. Web. Accessed 8 Aug. 2018.

Brooker, Joseph. *Literature of the 1980s: After the Watershed, Volume 9*. Edinburgh: Edinburgh University Press, 2010. Print.

Brown, Greg. 'Englaland by Steve Ely'. *World Literature Today*. 2016. Web. Accessed 9 Feb. 2018.

Buchan, Peter. *Ancient Ballads and Songs of the North of Scotland*. Edinburgh: W. Paterson, 1875. Print.

Busby, Nicole, and Rebecca Zahn. 'Women's Labour and Trade Unionism'. *Dangerous Women Project*. 2016. Web. Accessed 3 Apr. 2018.

Butts-Thompson, Natalie, and Deborah Price. *How Black Were Our Valleys: A 30 Year Commemoration of the 1984/85 Miners' Strike*. n.p: CreateSpace Independent Publishing, 2014. Print.

Carter, Sarah. '"Not Perfect Boy nor Perfect Wench": Ovid's Hermaphroditus and the Early Modern Hermaphrodite'. *The Survival Of Myth: Innovation, Singularity and Alterity*. Eds. David Kennedy and Paul Hardwick. Cambridge: Cambridge Scholars Publishing, 2010: 90–109. Print.

Carver, Terrell. *The Postmodern Marx*. Manchester: University of Manchester Press, 1998. Print.

Chesshyre, Robert. 'The Villages of the North Where the Pits Closed, But the Wounds Haven't'. *Independent*. 2013. Web. Accessed 1 June 2017.

Clegg, Richard. *Labour Disputes in the UK: 2016*. Office for National Statistics. 2017.

Clegg, Richard. *Labour Disputes in the UK: 2018*. Office for National Statistics. 2019.

Cohen, Nick. 'Don't Look to Len McCluskey and His Sorry Ilk to Defend Workers' Interests'. *Guardian*. 2018. Web. Accessed 27 Mar. 2018.

Colens, R. '1984'. *Against All the Odds*. Eds. Maurice Jones and William Ross. Sheffield: National Union of Mineworkers, 1984: 2–3. Print.

Constantine, David. *The Bloodaxe Book of Poetry Quotations*. Ed. Dennis O'Driscoll. Tarset: Bloodaxe, 2006: 169. Print.

Dabb, Tony. 'World War 2: 50th Anniversary. Official Secrets'. *Socialist Review*. 185. April 1995. Web. Accessed 3 Apr. 2018.

Davitt, Jack. 'The Big Fight'. *Against All the Odds*. Eds. Maurice Jones and William Ross. Sheffield: National Union of Mineworkers, 1984: 10–12. Print.
'Dead Miners "Never Be Forgotten"'. *BBC News*. 2009. Web. Accessed 1 May 2018.
Dean, Paul. 'History versus Poetry: The Battle of "Maldon"'. *Neuphilologische Mitteilungen* 93.1 (1992): 99–108. Print.
Dent, Shirley. 'Shirley Dent on How Literature Reflects the 1984 Miners' Strike'. *Guardian*. 2009. Web. Accessed 27 Apr. 2018.
Department for Business, Energy and Industrial Strategy. *Historical Coal Data: Coal Production, Availability and Consumption 1853 to 2015*. 2016. Print.
Department for Business, Energy and Industrial Strategy. *Trade Union Membership 2021: Statistical Bulletin*. London: Department for Business, Energy and Industrial Strategy. 2022. Print.
Department of Energy and Climate Change. *Historical Electricity Data: 1920 to 2012*. 2013. Print. Electricity Statistics.
Duncan, Andrew. 'Revolt in the Backlands: *Black Torch* Book One and the Silenced Voices of History'. *Reading Barry MacSweeney*. Ed. Paul Batchelor. Hexham: Bloodaxe, 2013: 63–75. Print.
Duncan, Robert, and Eric Mottram. 'Mottram to Duncan, 1 May 1972'. *The Unruly Garden: Robert Duncan and Eric Mottram Letters and Essays*. Eds. Amy Evans and Shamoon Zamir. Oxford: Peter Lang, 2007: 70–8. Print.
Dwyer, Owen J., and Derek H. Alderman. 'Memorial Landscapes: Analytic Questions and Metaphors'. *GeoJournal* 73.3 (2008): 165–78. Print.
Eagleton, Terry. 'Antagonisms: Tony Harrison's *V*.'. *Bloodaxe Critical Anthologies: Tony Harrison*. Ed. Neil Astley. Newcastle: Bloodaxe, 1991: 348–50. Print.
Eldridge, John, and Lizzie Eldridge. *Raymond Williams: Making Connections*. London: Routledge, 1994. MOBI File.
Ely, Steve. *Digging the Seam: Popular Cultures of the 1984/5 Miners' Strike*. Eds. Ian W. MacDonald and Simon Popple. Newcastle: Cambridge Scholars Publishing, 2012. Print.
Ely, Steve. *Englalaland*. Ripon: Smokestack, 2015. Print.
Ely, Steve. *Oswald's Book of Hours*. Middlesbrough: Smokestack, 2013. Print.
Ely, Steve. 'Tales of the Tribe: Modern Epic, Guerrilla-Pastoral and Utopian Yeoman-Anarchism in Oswald's Book of Hours and Englaland'. Doctoral Thesis. University of Huddersfield, 2016. Web. Accessed 24 Jul. 2018.
Ely, Steve, and Sheenagh Pugh. 'Interview with Steve Ely'. Sheenaghpugh. livejournal.com. 2015. Web. Accessed 7 Feb. 2018.
Ely, Steve, and Zack Wilson. 'Steve Ely: Poet of Sunday Leagues and Sainted Rebellion'. Zackwilsonlonestriker.blogspot.co.uk. 2012. Web. Accessed 9 Feb. 2018.
Engels, Friedrich. *The Condition of the Working Class in England in 1844*. Trans. Florence Kelley Wischnewetzky. New York: Cosimo, 2009. Print.
Erll, Astrid. *Memory in Culture*. Trans. Sara B. Young. Basingstoke: Palgrave Macmillan, 2011. Print.
'EU Referendum Results'. *BBC News*. 2016. Web. Accessed 12 Apr. 2018.

Bibliography

Field, John. 'Making History: Writings from the British Coalfields, 1984–5'. *Radical History Review* 38 (1987): 135–42. Print.

Feinstein, Elaine. *Ted Hughes: The Life of a Poet*. New York: W.W. Norton, 2001. Print.

Figgis, Mike. *The Battle of Orgreave*. UK: Artangel, 2001. Film.

Forché, Carolyn. 'Introduction'. *Against Forgetting: Twentieth-Century Poetry of Witness*. Ed. Carolyn Forché. New York and London: Norton, 1993: 29–47. Print.

Fowler, Alastair. 'Proper Naming: Personal Names in Literature'. *Essays in Criticism* 58.2 (2008): 97–119. Print.

Frow. R., E. Frow and Michael Katanka. *Strikes: A Documentary History*. London: Charles Knight and Co., 1971. Print.

Fryer, Bob. 'Trade Unionism in Crisis: the Miners' Strike and the Challenge to Union Democracy'. *Digging Deeper: Issues in the Miners' Strike*. Ed. Huw Beynon. London: Verso, 1985: 69–85. Print.

Gibbon, Peter, and David Steyne. *Thurcroft, A Village and the Miners' Strike: An Oral History*. Nottingham: Spokesman, 1986. Print.

Gittins, Jean. 'A Sad Tale of a Striker's Bride'. 1in12.com. Web. Accessed 7 Feb. 2018.

Gittins, Jean. 'Why Mam, Why?' 1in12.com. Web. Accessed 7 Feb. 2018.

Gittins, Jean. 'The Yorkshire Picket Song'. 1in12.com. Web. Accessed 7 Feb. 2018.

Goss, Richard. 'Renowned Estate Sells for £16M'. *East Anglian Daily Times*. 2010. Web. Accessed 19 Jan. 2017.

Grice, Andrew. 'Lord Parkinson's Secretary Claimed He "Begged" Her to Have an Abortion'. *Independent*. 2016. Web. Accessed 19 Jan. 2017.

Gunn, Thom. 'Ben Johnson'. *The Occasions of Poetry: Essays in Criticism and Autobiography*. Ed. Clive Wilmer. London: Faber and Faber, 1982: 106–17. Print.

Hale, William. 'The Future Belongs to the White Race'. *The Atlantic*. 2014. Web. Accessed 22 Mar. 2017.

Hall, Edith. 'Tony Harrison's Prometheus: A View from the Left'. *Arion* 10.1 (2002): 129–40. Print.

Harris, John. 'In Search of Arthur Scargill: 30 Years after the Miners' Strike'. *Guardian*. 2014. Web. Accessed 24 Oct. 2016.

Harrison, Tony. *The Inky Digit of Defiance: Selected Prose 1966–2016*. London: Faber and Faber, 2017. Print.

Harrison, Tony. 'Medea: A Sex-War Opera'. *Theatre Works: 1973–1985*. London: Penguin, 1986: 363–448. Print.

Harrison, Tony. 'The Oresteia'. *Theatre Works: 1973–1985*. London: Penguin, 1986: 185–292. Print.

Harrison, Tony. *Permanently Bard*. Ed. Carol Rutter. Newcastle upon Tyne: Bloodaxe Books, 1995. Print.

Harrison, Tony. *Plays One: The Mysteries*. London: Faber and Faber, 1999. Print.

Harrison, Tony. *Prometheus*. London: Faber and Faber, 1998. Print.

Harrison, Tony. *V.* Northumberland: Bloodaxe, 2008. Print.

Hargreaves, A.S. 'Artifices, Statute of'. *The Oxford Companion to British History* (1st rev. ed.). Oxford: Oxford University Press, 2009. Web. Accessed 23 March. 2018.

Harvie, Jen. *Staging the UK*. Manchester and New York: Manchester University Press, 2005. Print.

Heffer, Simon. 'The Dockers, Churchill and the War's Most Shameful Secret: Second World War Strikes Reveal Disgusting Lack of Patriotism'. *Daily Mail*. 30 January 2015. Print.

Hegel, Georg Wilhelm Friedrich. 'Poetry'. *Aesthetics: Lectures on Fine Art*. Trans. T.M. Knox. Oxford: Clarendon Press, 1975: 959–99. Print.

Hélie, Claire. 'From Picket Lines to Poetic Ones: the 1984–1985 Miners' Strike and the Idea of a "Condition of England Poetry"'. *Études britanniques contemporaines* 49 (2015). Web. Accessed 28 Jan. 2018.

Herbert, George. 'The Collar'. *The Norton Anthology Of Poetry*. Eds. Margaret Ferguson, Mary Jo Salter and Jon Stallworthy. New York: Norton, 2005: 379. Print.

Herbert, W.N. 'Barry MacSweeney and the Demons of Influence: *Pearl* and *The Book of Demons*'. *Reading Barry MacSweeney*. Ed. Paul Batchelor. Hexham: Bloodaxe, 2013: 141–56. Print.

Herbert, W.N. and Matthew Hollis. 'Sean O'Brien'. *Strong Words: Modern Poets on Modern Poetry*. Eds. W.N Herbert and Matthew Hollis. Tarset: Bloodaxe, 2000: 236–40. Print.

'The History of Strikes in the UK'. Office for National Statistics. 2015. Web. Accessed 24 Jul. 2018.

Howells, Kim. 'Stopping Out: The Birth of a New Kind of Politics'. *Digging Deeper: Issues in the Miners' Strike*. Ed. Huw Beynon. London: Verso, 1985: 139–48. Print.

Hughes, Ted. *The Spoken Word: Ted Hughes: Poems and Short Stories*. London: British Library Board, 2008. CD.

Hughes, Ted. *Collected Poems of Ted Hughes*. Ed. Paul Keegan. London: Faber and Faber, 2005. Print.

Hughes, Ted. *Letters of Ted Hughes*. Ed. Christopher Reid. London: Faber and Faber, 2007. Print.

Hundal, Sunny. 'Operation Blue Star: 25 Years On'. *The Guardian*. 2009. Web. Accessed 8 Dec. 2015.

Inglis, Fred. 'End of an Epoch'. *Raymond Williams*. London: Routledge, 1998: 260–88. Print.

Institute for Public Policy Research. *Fall In Trade Union Membership Linked To Rising Share Of Income Going To Top 1%*. 2018. Web. Accessed 13 Aug. 2018.

'IPCC Sorry for Orgreave Probe Delay'. *BBC News*. 2014. Web. 18 Aug. 2014.

@IWGBUniveristyLondon. 'As @UoLondon have not had the courtesy to reply to @IWGBunion workers campaigning to be brought in-house, the workers have been writing directly to Vice-Chancellor Adrian Smith—see below for a fantastic indictment of #outsourcing from IHR receptionist Glen Jacques!' Twitter. 20 June 2018, 2.25a.m. Web. Accessed 13 Aug. 2018.

Jenkins, Maureen. 'Some Day They'll Understand'. *Against All the Odds*. Eds. Maurice Jones and William Ross. Sheffield: National Union of Mineworkers, 1984: 47–8. Print.

Johnson, Linton Kwesi. Lyrics to 'It Dread Inna Inglan'. Lyrics.com. N.d. Web. Accessed 14 May 2022.

Jones, Maurice. 'Foreword'. *Against All the Odds*. Eds. Maurice Jones and William Ross. Sheffield: National Union of Mineworkers, 1984: 1. Print.

Jones, Maurice, and William Ross, eds. *Against All the Odds*. Sheffield: National Union of Mineworkers, 1984. Print.

Jones, Nicholas. *Strikes and the Media*. Oxford: Blackwell, 1986. Print.

Jones, Owen. *Chavs: The Demonization of the Working Class*. London: Verso, 2012. Print.

Jones, Richard H. 'Review: "The Battle Of Maldon A.D. 91"'. *Albion: A Quarterly Journal Concerned with British Studies* 24.2 (1992): 297–9. Print.

Kelly, Gavin, and Daniel Tomlinson. 'The Future of Trade Unionism and the Next Generation'. *What is the Future of British Trade Unionism: Radix Paper Number 4*. Ed. Nick Tyrone. London: Radix, 2016: 10–15. Print.

Klepuszewski, Wojciech. 'V. – Tony Harrison's Poetic Dialectic'. *Lingua* 21 (2011): 21–32. Print.

Kunkel, Benjamin. *Utopia or Bust: A Guide to the Present Crisis*. London and New York: Verso, 2014. Print.

'Labour Disputes;UK;Sic 07;Total Working Days Lost;All Inds. and Services (000'S)'. Ons.gov.uk. 2018. Web. Accessed 3 Apr. 2018.

Laybourn, Keith. *The General Strike of 1926*. Manchester: Manchester University Press, 1993. Print.

Littleton, Suellen M. *The Wapping Dispute*. Aldershot: Avebury, 1992. Print.

MacSweeney, Barry. '[475] Barry MacSweeney: Note'. *Certain Prose: The English Intelligencer*. Eds. Neil Pattison, Reitha Pattison and Luke Roberts. Cambridge: Mountain, 2014: 145–6. Print.

MacSweeney, Barry. 'Barry MacSweeney Reads a Selection of Poems from His Book *Black Torch*'. Writers at Warwick Archive. 2019. Web. Accessed 31 Mar 2020.

MacSweeney, Barry. *Black Torch*. London: New London Pride, 1978. Print.

MacSweeney, Barry. *Wolf Tongue: Selected Poems 1965–2000*. Tarset: Bloodaxe Books, 2003. Print.

Marine Scotland. *Scottish Government Response to the European Commission's Green Paper on Reform of the Common Fisheries Policy*. Edinburgh: Marine Scotland, 2009. Print.

Massey, Doreen. 'Places and Their Pasts'. *History Workshop Journal* 39.1 (1995): 182–92. Print.

Masterman, Len. 'The Battle of Orgreave'. *Television Mythologies*. London: Comedia, 1984: 99–109. Print.

McCann, Kate. 'Labour "Would Take the Country Back to the 1970s" with Trade Union Membership in Every Workplace'. *Telegraph*. 2017. Web. Accessed 17 Apr. 2018.

McMillan, J. 'They'll Never Smash the NUM'. *Against All The Odds*. Eds. Maurice Jones and William Ross. Sheffield: National Union of Mineworkers, 1984: 16–17. Print.

McSmith, Andy. *No Such Thing As Society: A History of Britain in the 1980s*. London: Constable, 2011. Print.

McVeigh, Karen. 'Grimethorpe, The Mining Village That Hit Rock Bottom—Then Bounced Back'. *Guardian*. 2015. Web. Accessed 11 Aug. 2017.

Metropolitan Police. 'Metropolitan Police Service—MPS Publication Scheme—Blair Peach'. Met.police.uk. 2010. Web. Accessed 15 Jan. 2016.

Milne, Seumas. *The Enemy Within: The Secret War against the Miners*. London and New York: Verso, 2014. Print.

'Miners' strike 1984–85: "A Civil War Without Guns"'. Socialistparty.org.uk. 2004. Web. Accessed 8 Dec. 2015.

Minkin, Lewis. *The Contentious Alliance: Trade Unions and the Labour Party*. Edinburgh: Edinburgh University Press, 1991. Print.

Moran, Alice, and Hannah Thompson. 'Public Sector Strikes'. YouGov. 2011. Web. Accessed 11 Apr. 2018.

Morgan, Bryn. 'General Election Results 1 May 1997'. Researchbriefings. parliament.uk. 1997. Web. Accessed 27 Mar. 2017.

Moritz, A.F. 'What Man Has Made Of Man'. *Poetry Foundation*. 2009. Web. Accessed 29 Nov. 2017.

Mort, Helen. *Division Street*. London: Chatto & Windus, 2013. Print.

Mort, Helen. 'My Town: Poet Helen Mort on Being Inspired by Sheffield'. *Yorkshire Post*. 2016. Web. Accessed 7 Feb. 2018.

Mort, Helen, and Rachael Allen. 'Helen Mort | Interview'. *Granta Magazine*. 2013. Web. Accessed 7 Feb. 2018.

Motion, Andrew. 'Andrew Motion on Retiring as Poet Laureate'. *Guardian*. 2009. Web. Accessed 17 May 2018.

'NUM: Historic Speeches'. Num.org.uk. 2015. Web. Accessed 20 Dec. 2015.

O'Brien, Sean. *The Beautiful Librarians*. London: Picador, 2015. Print.

O'Brien, Sean. *Collected Poems*. London: Picador, 2012. Print.

O'Brien, Sean. 'Contemporary British Poetry'. *A Companion to 20th-Century Poetry*. Ed. Neil Roberts. Oxford: Blackwell, 2003: 571–84. Print.

O'Brien, Sean. *The Deregulated Muse: Essays on Contemporary British and Irish Poetry*. Newcastle Upon Tyne: Bloodaxe, 1998. Print.

O'Brien, Sean. *The Frighteners*. Newcastle upon Tyne: Bloodaxe, 1987. Print.

O'Brien, Sean. 'Poetry Politics'. *The Bloodaxe Book of Poetry Quotations*. Ed. Dennis O'Driscoll. Tarset: Bloodaxe, 2006: 172. Print.

'Occasional Poem'. *Poetry Foundation*. Web. Accessed 2 Nov. 2017.

O'Cofaigh, C.B. 'We Are the Future'. *Against All the Odds*. Eds. Maurice Jones and William Ross. Sheffield: National Union of Mineworkers, 1984: 38–9. Print.

O'Connor, Danny. *Ted Hughes and Trauma*. London: Palgrave Macmillan, 2016. Print.

Bibliography

'Olivier Winners 1985'. *Official London Theatre*. Web. Accessed 24 July 2018.

Padley, Steve. '"Hijacking Culture": Tony Harrison and the Greeks'. *Cycnos* 18.1 (2001): n.pag. Print.

Paterson, Harry. *Look Back in Anger: The Miners' Strike in Nottinghamshire—30 Years On*. Nottingham: Five Leaves, 2014. Print.

Petkova, Yanitsa. *Contracts that Do Not Guarantee a Minimum Number of Hours: April 2018*. London: Office For National Statistics, 2018. Print.

Philo, Greg. *Really Bad News*. London: Writers and Readers, 1982. Print.

Proshansky, Harold, M. Abbe K. Fabian, and Robert Kaminoff. 'Place-Identity: Physical World Socialization of the Self'. *The People, Place, and Space Reader*. Eds. Jen Jack Gieseking et al. New York: Routledge, 2014: 77–81. Print.

'Public Sector Strike Rallies Held Across UK'. *BBC News*. 2011. Web. Accessed 11 Apr. 2018.

Pugh, Sheenagh. 'Review of *Englaland* by Steve Ely'. Sheenaghpugh.livejournal.com. 2015. Web. Accessed 9 Feb. 2018.

Ramdin, Ron. *The Making of the Black Working Class in Britain*. London: Verso, 2017. Print.

Reddish, Eileen. 'England—1984'. *Against All the Odds*. Eds. Maurice Jones and William Ross. Sheffield: National Union of Mineworkers, 1984: 5. Print.

Richards, Andrew John. *Miners on Strike*. Oxford: Berg, 1996. Print.

Riley, Peter. 'Poets, Angry'. *The Fortnightly Review*. 2015. Web. Accessed 9 Feb. 2018.

Riley, Peter. 'Thoughts on Barry MacSweeney'. *Reading Barry MacSweeney*. Ed. Paul Batchelor. Hexham: Bloodaxe, 2013: 131–40. Print.

Roberts, Jayne. '1984'. *Against All the Odds*. Eds. Maurice Jones and William Ross. Sheffield: National Union of Mineworkers, 1984: 43–4. Print.

Roberts, Luke. *Seditious Things: Barry MacSweeney and the Politics of Post-War British Poetry*. Cham: Palgrave MacMillan, 2017. Print.

Rogaly, Joe. *Grunwick*. Middlesex: Penguin, 1977. Print.

Rogers, Roy. 'Defiant Scargill Set to Ignore Court Writ'. *Glasgow Herald*. 1984: 1. Web. Accessed 7 Jan. 2016.

Rubin, David C. 'Introduction'. *Memory In Oral Traditions: The Cognitive Psychology of Epic, Ballads, and Counting-Out Rhymes*. Oxford: Oxford University Press, 1995: 3–14. Print.

Sajé, Natasha. 'Poetry and Ethics: Writing about Others'. Awpwriter.org. 2009. Web. Accessed 21 Jan. 2019.

Samuel, Raphael. 'Introduction'. *The Enemy Within: Pit Villages and the Miners' Strike of 1984–5*. Eds. Raphael Samuel, Barbara Bloomfield and Guy Boanas. London: Routledge and Kegan Paul, 1986: 1–39. Print.

Scargill, Arthur, and Joanne Corcoran. 'I Fought the Law – Talking to Arthur Scargill 20 Years After the Miners' Strike'. Anphoblacht.com. 2005. Web. Accessed 21 Nov. 2016.

Schechner, Richard. *Performance Studies: An Introduction*. London: Routledge, 2006. Print.

Secretary of State for Employment. *Report of a Court of Inquiry under the RT Hon Lord Justice Scarman, OBE into a Dispute between Grunwick Processing Laboratories Limited and Members of the Association of Professional, Executive, Clerical and Computer Staff.* London: Her Majesty's Stationery Office, 1977. Print.

Shaheen, Faiza. 'In the Gig Economy, Recruitment Agencies Are the Gangmasters'. *Guardian.* 2016. Web. Accessed 15 Aug. 2017.

Shaw, Katy. *Mining the Meaning: Cultural Representations of the 1984–5 UK Miners' Strike.* Newcastle upon Tyne: Cambridge Scholars, 2012. Print.

Shaw, Katy. '(Re)Writing the 1984–5 UK Miners' Strike: Poetry and Politics 1985–2015'. *London Economic.* 2015. Web. Accessed 7 Feb. 2018.

Sider, Theodore. *Four-Dimensionalism: An Ontology of Persistence and Time.* Oxford: Clarendon Press, 2001. Print.

Simms, Bill. 'To a Bottom One'. *Against All the Odds.* Eds. Maurice Jones and William Ross. Sheffield: National Union of Mineworkers, 1984: 2. Print.

Sinfield, Alan. *Literature, Politics and Culture in Postwar Britain.* London: Continuum, 2007. Print.

Smith, David, and Sabrina Siddiqui. 'Donald Trump Tells CPAC: "We Are Americans and the Future Belongs to Us"'. *Guardian.* 2017. Web. Accessed 22 Mar. 2017.

Soldon, Norbert C. 'British Women and Trade Unionism: Opportunities Made and Missed'. *The World of Women's Trade Unionism.* Ed. Norbert C. Soldon. Westport: Greenwood Press, 1985: 11–33. Print.

Sontag, Susan. *Regarding the Pain of Others.* London: Penguin, 2003. MOBI File.

Stephenson, Carol, and Jean Spence. 'Pies and Essays: Women Writing through the British 1984–1985 Coal Miners' Strike'. *Gender, Place & Culture: A Journal of Feminist Geography* (2012): 1–18. Print.

Stewart, Matthew. 'Largo—Paul Bentley'. *Sphinx Review.* 2012. Web. Accessed 26 Sept. 2016.

'Strike Is a Damp Squib—Cameron'. *BBC News.* 2011. Web. Accessed 11 Apr. 2018.

'Striking Stuff by Jean A. Gittins'. 1in12.com. Web. Accessed 7 Feb. 2018.

Sugano, Marian Zwerling. *The Poetics of the Occasion: Mallarme and the Poetry of Circumstance.* Stanford: Stanford University Press, 1992. Print.

Tarver, Nick. '"Battle of Orgreave" Remembered'. *BBC News.* 2014. Web. Accessed 18 Aug. 2014.

Taylor, Robert. *The TUC: From the General Strike to New Unionism.* Basingstoke: Palgrave Macmillan, 2000. Print.

Thatcher, Margaret. 'Remarks on Becoming Prime Minister (St Francis's Prayer)'. Margaretthatcher.org. N.d. Web. Accessed 2 Aug. 2018.

Thompson, E.P. *The Making of the English Working Class.* Middlesex: Penguin, 1968. Print.

Trade Union Act 2016, c.15. Legislation.gov.org. 2016. Web. Accessed 12 Apr. 2018.

'Trade Union Act Becomes Law'. Gov.uk. 2016. Web. Accessed 12 Apr. 2018.

'Trade Unions: The Current List and Schedule'. Gov.uk. 2018. Web. Accessed 14 Sept. 2018.

Travis, Alan. 'National Archives: Margaret Thatcher Wanted to Crush Power of Trade Unions'. *Guardian*. 2013. Web. Accessed 4 Apr. 2018.

Uetricht, Micah. *Strike for America: Chicago Teachers against Austerity*. London and New York: Verso, 2014. Print.

'Vote 2001: Results and Constituencies: Hartlepool'. *BBC News*. 2001. Web. Accessed 19 Jan. 2017.

Walker, Monica. 'Tell it to the Children'. *Against All the Odds*. Eds. Maurice Jones and William Ross. Sheffield: National Union of Mineworkers, 1984: 28–9. Print.

Warner, Kimberly, et al. *National Seafood Fraud Testing Results Highlights*. Oceana. org. 2013. Web. Accessed 2 Dec. 2016.

Watson-Smyth, Kate. 'Tory Adviser Plans Pyramid Mausoleum'. *Independent*. 2000. Web. Accessed 19 Jan. 2017.

Weaver, Matthew. 'The Gordon Brown and Gillian Duffy Transcript'. *Guardian*. 2010. Web. Accessed 14 May 2022.

White, Michael. 'Margaret Thatcher: Looking Back on the Life of the Iron Lady'. *Guardian*. 2013. Web. Accessed 25 Jul. 2019.

Willey, Stephen. 'Bob Cobbing 1950–1978: Performance, Poetry and the Institution'. Doctoral thesis. Queen Mary, University of London, 2012. Web. Accessed 24 Jul. 2018.

Williams, Raymond. *Keywords: A Vocabulary of Culture and Society*. London: Fontana, 1989a. Print.

Williams, Raymond. *Marxism and Literature*. Oxford: Oxford University Press, 1977. Print.

Williams, Raymond. *Resources of Hope*. Ed. Robin Gable. London: Verso, 1989b. Print.

Winterton, Jonathan, and Ruth Winterton. *Coal, Crisis, and Conflict: The 1984–85 Miners' Strike in Yorkshire*. Manchester: Manchester University Press, 1989. Print.

Woodcock, Bruce. 'Poet as Heretic: the Political Imagination of Sean O'Brien'. *Critical Survey* 10.1 (1998): 33–58. Print.

Wright, David. 'The National Fire Strike Ten Years On'. *FIRE*. 2012. Web. Accessed 11 Apr. 2018.

Index

Abercrombie, Nicholas 52
Aeschylus 98–9
Against all the Odds 20, 109–15, 123–4
Alderman, Derek 77
Alexander, Elizabeth 6n4
Amis, Martin 88
Armitage, Simon 102, 126
Aronowitz, Stanley 50
Aske, Robert 77
Asos 106
Auden, W.H. 8

Ball, John 77n5
Bate, Jonathan 117, 119n8, 120n9, 123
Baudrillard, Jean 60
BBC 36–9
Beckett, Francis 23, 24, 26, 29, 30, 39n3, 47
Beharell, Peter 38n
Bell, Bethan 29
Bentley, Paul
   community 91, 92–103, 108, 128
   focus on 9, 91
   Largo 14–15, 68, 97
   miners' strike (1984–5) 92–103, 114, 128
   poetry reading 110n2
   Scargill and 68–71, 92–3, 122
   'Two Magicians' 14–15, 68–71, 92–103, 121–2, 125–6, 128
   women and 17
Berger, John 97, 125
Bernstein, Charles 126

Betjeman, John 116–17, 118
Billy Elliot (film) 104n, 106, 107
Blair, Tony 73
Bloodworth, James 18, 23
Brassed Off (film) 103–4, 105, 106, 107, 108, 127
Brexit referendum (2016) 33
British Leyland 37n2
Brody, Richard 107
Bromley, George 28
Brooker, Joseph 75
Brown, Gordon 53
Brown, Jack 122
Busby, Nicole 27
Butts-Thompson, Natalie 62, 95n3

Callaghan, James 29
Cameron, David 32
Carroll, Lewis 65
Carter, Sarah 88
Carver, Terrell 106
Chesshyre, Robert 92
children and poetry 113–14
Citrine, Walter 24
Cohen, Nick 4
Colens, R. 113
Collins, Jack 47
communities
   Bentley 91, 92–103, 108
   Ely 91, 106–7, 108
   history and place 91–2, 108
   identity 105
   Mort 91, 103–8

Index

politics 96
strikes and 91–108
Thurcroft 93–102, 108, 128
Connell, Joe 52
Coogan, Steve 35
Courtaulds Red Scar Mill 27–8
Cunningham, Mary 3

Dabb, Tony 25
Davitt, Jack 113
Dean, Paul 84
Deller, Jeremy 59, 60, 104, 127
Dent, Shirley 111
Desai, Jayaben 29
Dismas the Good Thief 77n5
Donaldson, Ian Stuart 85
Doody, Dennis 52, 53, 54
Duffy, Gillian 53
Duncan, Andrew 36
Duncan, Robert 110n2
Dwyer, Owen 77

Eagleton, Terry 1, 11
Easington Colliery 92
Eldridge, Lizzie and John 66
Ely, Steve
'Arthur Scargill' 16, 30–1
'Ballad of Dave Hart' 79, 82
'Ballad of the Scabs' 24, 48–51, 55, 56, 79, 82–3, 86, 128–9
community 91, 106–7, 108
Englaland 15–16, 48, 79, 82, 83, 87
focus on 9, 15–16, 91
'Harrowing of the North' 48, 87
'Inglan is a Bitch' 52, 53–4, 88
'Irish Blood, English Heart' 51–4
'It Dread Inna Inglan' 53
miners' strike (1984–5) 77–89, 127–9
'Nithing' 18, 79, 86–7, 128
'Objective One' 106–7
'One of Us' 79, 83, 88
Oswald's Book of Hours 15–16, 77
poetic moment 48–54
Scargill and 15, 16, 18, 30–1, 77–89, 128
'Scum of the Earth' 79, 83–5, 128–9
Thatcher and 18, 53, 79, 80–1, 83–4, 86–9
TUC and 62
women and 16–17

employment, precariousness 2, 105, 106
environmental protection 123
equal pay 16, 27, 104n
ethnic minorities 16n11, 27–9

Falkland War (1982) 30, 125
Faulkner, William 15
Feinstein, Elaine 117
Field, John 110
films 27, 103–8, 127
firefighters 31–2
Forché, Carolyn 17, 116
Ford Sewing Machinists' Strike (1968) 16, 27, 104n
Fortune, Pat 96
Fowler, Alastair 68
France, 1968 riots 36–7, 38
Francis, Richard 37
Francis of Assisi, Saint 71, 73–4
Fryer, Bob 94–5
Full Monty, The (film) 104n, 105, 106, 107

Galloway, George 85, 86
Gandhi, Indira 42
General Strike (1926) 24, 113
Gibbon, Peter, *Thurcroft* 14, 93–102, 108, 128
Ginsberg, Allan 37
Gittins, Jean 114–16
Greek drama 98–9
Green, Joe 112–13
Griffin, Nick 15, 85, 86
Griffiths, David 62
Grunwick Strike (1976) 16, 28–9
Gunn, Thom 7–8

Hamburger, Michael 123
Hanson, Lord 51, 82–3
Harold Godwinson, King 86–7
Harrison, Tony
class 41, 43, 46, 62, 79
Doomsday 12
dramatic works 12, 98–9
education 44
focus on 9, 11–13, 126
From the School of Eloquence 44
miners' strike (1984–5) 36, 40–6, 111, 126, 127–8
narrative 18

Nativity 12
Passion 12
poetry reading 110n2
positionality 42
Scargill and 11–12, 40, 41, 45
'Them and uz' 44, 67
'V' 11–12, 40–6, 81, 111, 125, 126
Harvie, Jen 58, 59–60, 61
Heath, Edward 10, 26, 49
Heffer, Simon 25
Hegel, Georg 7
Hélie, Claire 114, 116
Hencke, David 23, 24, 26, 29, 30, 39
Henry VIII 77n5
Herbert, George 69–70
Herbert, W.N. 13, 71
Herman, Mark 103–4
hermaphroditism 88
Hollis, Matthew 13
Howells, Kim 95n3
Hughes, Olwyn 119n8
Hughes, Ted
  'Best Worker in Europe' 109, 120–2
  biographies 117
  Birthday Letters 117
  environmental protection and 123
  miners' strike (1984–5) and 122, 123
  'On the Reservations' 117–18
  poet laureate 20, 117–24
  'Rain-Charm for the Duchy' 120
  River 120
  Wolfwatching 117–18

India 42
Indian Workers Association 28
individualism 33, 96, 114, 121
industrial decline 12, 13, 20, 104–5, 108, 112
Industrial Revolution 92
inequality 3, 13
Inglis, Fred 66
Institute for Public Policy Research (IPPR) 3
International Women's Strikes 17
Iraq 32

Jacques, Glen 2
Johnson, Linton Kwesi 52, 53
Johnson, Wayne 77n5
Jones, David 112–13

Jones, Jack 38n
Jones, Maurice, *Against all the Odds* 109–16, 123–4, 128
Jones, Owen 3, 24, 35, 59, 105
Joseph the Dreamer 77n5

Keats, John 69
Kelly, Gavin 4
Kinnock, Neil 66n1
Kipling, Rudyard 84
Klepuszewski, Wojcjech 41–2
Kripke, Saul 68
Kunkel, Benjamin 71, 78

Laing, Hector 51, 82–3
Laird, Nick 1
Larkin, Philip 119
Lindo, George 53
Lucas, John 121
Lydon, John 71

McAllister, Andrew 13n9
McCann, Kate 33
MacGregor, Ian 30, 41, 43, 44, 45–6, 86, 113
McMillan, J. 113
McPhee, Don 15, 55
McSmith, Andy 30, 57
MacSweeney, Barry
  1974 miners' strike 36
  Black Torch 36–40
  'Black Torch Sunrise' 10–11, 24, 36–40, 127
  'Colonel B' 73
  focus on 9–11, 126
  'John Bunyan to Johnny Rotten' 10, 71–4
  narrative 18
  'Persuasion' 127
  Scargill and 10, 71–4
  'Shells Her Auburn Hair Did Show' 127
  Thatcher and 10, 71, 73–4
  TUC and 62
  Wolf Tongue 10
Made in Dagenham (film) 27, 104n, 106–7
Mahmood, Shabnam 29
Major, John 73
Maldon, Battle of (991) 83–4

Index

Malley, Kev 52
Manchester Arena attack (2017) 7n
Mandelson, Peter 15, 83, 84, 85–6, 128
Mao Zedong 78
Marr, Johnny 69, 92
Marx, Karl 78
Mary Magdalene 77n5
Massey, Doreen 91, 92, 108
Mayakovsky, Vladimir 9n6
memorials 77, 78
memory 15, 57, 58, 77, 98
Michael, Archangel 77n5
Milne, Seumas 29, 30, 58, 61
Minden, Battle of (1759) 83–4
miners' strike (1984–5)
    army and 62
    Bentley on 14, 92–103, 128
    cultural appropriation 91
    defining moment 110
    Ely on 77–89, 127–9
    Harrison and 11–12, 40–6, 111, 126, 127–8
    Hughes and 122, 123
    legacy 5, 15, 57–62, 65–6, 100, 103, 109, 114
    Mort on 15, 55–63, 127–8
    motivations 31
    naming Scargill and Thatcher 20, 65–89
    O'Brien on 13, 46–8, 74–6, 126–7
    'official' poetry responses 109–24
    poetic responses 36
    politics 30
    Thatcher *see* Thatcher, Margaret
    Thurcroft 14, 93–102, 108, 128
    war discourse 30, 43
    women and 17
miners' strikes
    1972/74 11, 26, 36, 49–50, 110n2
    1984 *see* miners' strike (1984–5)
    Durham (1844) 10
    effect 2
    history 23–4, 26–7
    period 5
Minkin, Lewis 95n3
Mitchell, Andrew 13–14
Moritz, A.F. 8
Mort, Helen
    communities 91, 103–8
    Division Street 15, 55, 103
    focus on 9, 91
    miners' strike (1984–5) 15, 55–63, 114, 127–8
    'Pit Closure as a Tarantino Short' 107, 108
    'Scab' 15, 20, 55–63, 81, 103–7, 108, 127
    women and 17, 58
Motion, Andrew 66n1, 117
Mottram, Eric 36, 110n2
Murdoch, Rupert 31
Myers, Lucas 118

naming politics 20, 65–89
narratives
    BBC 36–9
    construction 6, 60, 62, 63, 65, 126–9
    control 66, 74–5
    function 5–6
    gender and 19
    industrial decline 20
    naming 65–6
    negotation 63
    trade unions 4, 33–4
    war 30, 43, 84, 125
Nellist, Dave 85
neoliberalism 33, 121
Nevison, John 77
Next PLC 106
nuclear energy 30, 33n7

Obama, Barack 6n4
O'Brien, Mick 52
O'Brien, Sean
    'Another Country' 13
    Beautiful Librarian 13
    'Cousin Coat' 46
    focus on 9, 13–14, 126
    Frighteners 46–8, 74, 75
    Hughes and 118
    Indoor Park 13
    'London Road' 46, 125
    miners' strike (1984–5) 13, 36, 46–8, 74–6, 126–7
    narrative 18, 62
    poetry and politics 129
    Scargill and 74–6
    'Summertime' 46–8, 75, 126–7
    'Unregistered' 74–6
occasional poetry 6–8

Index

O'Cofaigh, C.B. 114
O'Connor, Danny 121
oral history 14, 93, 95, 101
Orgreave, Battle of 17, 55, 57, 59, 60–2, 127
Oswald, King of Northumbria 77n5
outsourcing 2

Padley, Steve 99
Parkinson, Cecil 79–81, 128
Partridge, Alan 35
Paterson, Harry 30
Paul, Saint 77n5
Paulin, Tom 121
Peach, Blair 51–2, 53–4
PEN Pinter Prize 12
Philo, Greg 37
Pickard, Tom 37, 110n2
Pilinsky, Jáos 118
place *see* communities
Plath, Sylvia 117
poetry
    function 6–9, 97, 125, 126
    politics and 1, 19–21
    see also individual poets
poets laureate 20–1, 116–24
politics
    naming 20, 65–89
    place 96
    poetry and 1, 19–21, 129
    poets laureate 116–24
Popa, Vasko 118
populism 85
postal workers 32
Price, Deborah 95n3
Pride (film) 104n, 106–7
Pugh, Sheenah 15–16

race 16n11, 27–9
Ramdin, Ron 27–8
Reddish, Eileen 111
Reid, Christopher 122
Resolution Foundation 4
Richardson, Richard 46–8
Ridley Report (1977) 74–5
Riley, Peter 19
Roberts, Jayne 113
Roberts, Luke 9, 11
Roberts, Michael Symmons 103
Roberts, Richard 28

Robin Hood 77n5
Rogaly, Joe 28
Rolle, Richard 77
Ross, William, *Against all the Odds* 109–16, 123–4
Rubin, David 68
rural community 66

Saddam Hussein 32
Sajé, Natasha 97
Scargill, Arthur
    1974 strike 26
    Against all the Odds and 113
    attempted assassination 87n13
    Bentley on 68–71, 92–3, 122
    Ely on 15, 16, 18, 30–1, 77–89, 128
    Harrison and 11–12, 40, 41, 45
    Hughes and 122
    'King Arthur' 68–74, 79, 80, 83, 92–3
    legacy 82
    London flat 81n7
    MacSweeney on 10, 71–4
    naming 20, 68–76
    O'Brien on 74–6
    prosecution 50–1
Schechner, Richard 60
Sex Pistols 71
Shakespeare, William 12
Shaw, Katy 17, 114, 116
Shelley, Percy Bysshe 109
Sider, Theodore 68
Simms, Bill 111–12
Sinfield, Alan 18, 61, 125
Smith, Adam 78
Smith, Adrian 2
Social Contract 39n3
Sontag, Susan 6, 97
Spence, Jean 17, 18, 19, 115
Stephenson, Carol 17, 18, 19, 115
Stewart, Matthew 14–15, 68–9
Steyne, David, *Thurcroft* 14, 93–102, 108, 128
strikes
    communities and 91–108
    historical list 5
    historical statistics 24–6
    miners *see* miners' strikes
    right to 4
    Winter of Discontent 29
Sugano, Marian 7

Index

Tarantino, Quentin 107
teachers 32
Tebbit, Norman 79n6
Tennyson, Alfred 14
Thatcher, Margaret
   Against all the Odds and 113
   attempted assassination 87
   biography 88
   election victory 29
   Ely on 18, 53, 79, 80–1, 83–4, 86–9
   'enemy within' 125
   energy policy 30
   gender and 88
   Hughes and 119, 121, 122, 123
   legacy 58
   MacSweeney on 10, 71, 73–4
   miners' strike and 29, 30
   Mort on 15, 58
   naming 20
   narratives 18
   O'Brien and 13
   resignation 118
   St Francis and 71, 73–4
   Wapping print dispute and 31
   war discourse 125
Thompson, E.P. 4, 28n4, 44
Thurcroft 14, 93–102, 108, 128
Tighe, Patrick 52, 53
Tolpuddle martyrs 113
Tomlinson, Daniel 4
trade unions
   20th-century history 23–34
   2016 Act 32–3
   decline 3–4, 9, 24, 29, 72, 129
   ethnic minorities and 27–9
   historical restrictions 3, 4–5
   moments 36
   narratives 4, 33–4
   public perception 4, 31–2
   role 2–3, 35
   women and 16–19, 25, 27
Trades Union Congress (TUC) 10, 16, 24, 27, 38–40, 51, 62, 82
tube drivers 32

Uetricht, Micah 3
unemployment 1–2, 31
United States 3, 6, 50

Walden, Brian 43
Walker, Monica 114
Walsh, Tony 7n
Wapping print dispute (1986–7) 31
war discourse 30, 43, 84, 125
Warde, Alan 52
Wellesley, Arthur, Duke of Wellington 15, 83, 84–5, 86, 128
Whitehurst, Billy 77n5
Wilhelm II, Kaiser 83n11
Wilkie, David 113n4
Willey, Stephen 10n6
William the Conqueror 48n6, 86–7
Williams, Raymond 6, 65–7, 70, 72–3, 81, 89
Wilson, Harold 26, 29, 37n2, 38n
women
   dramatic chorus 99
   Ely and 53
   equal pay 16, 27, 104n
   misogyny 88
   Mort and 17, 58
   narratives 19
   poetry on children 113–14
   trade unions and 16–19, 25, 27
Women Strike for Equality (1970) 17
Women Strike for Peace (1961) 17
Woodcock, Bruce 13–14
Wordsworth, William 8
Wright, David 32

Young, Hugo 88

Zahn, Rebecca 27
Zuboff, Shoshana 91

Printed and bound by CPI Group (UK) Ltd, Croydon, CR0 4YY
12/05/2024